Hello, South Korea

The rooftops of
Jeonju Hanok Village

Hello, South Korea

Meet the country behind Hallyu

목차

Contents

Right Seoul's skyline behind Bukchon Hanok Village

Below left The iconic pink guard costumes from *Squid Game*

Below right Korea's famed fried chicken

Welcome to South Korea

The world's biggest boy band, Netflix's most-watched series ever, the first non-English language film to bag a Best Picture Oscar – South Korea is a force to be reckoned with.

Korea's influence on the world cannot be overstated. K-everything is everywhere – across the globe, street performers dance to the bubblegum sounds of K-pop, supermarket shelves are stocked with kimchi and the beauty community clamours for the latest products straight out of Seoul. There's even a name for this phenomenon: Hallyu, the Korean Wave. Hallyu has made its mark on practically every country – and this wave shows no signs of breaking.

So Korea is all about pop culture, right? Wrong. Did you know that women have been free diving off of Jeju Island since the 17th century? That, until 2022, Koreans counted their age three different ways? Or that the country is a world leader in the field of archery, constantly dominating at competitions? Korea is so much more than its Hallyu parts, and it's time the world met the incredible country behind the headlines.

Hello, South Korea helps you do just that, introducing the beautiful landscapes, captivating history and time-honoured traditions that have shaped this spectacular nation. Along the way, you'll get to know the sumptuous foods, innovative arts scene and talented people at its very heart (including those global exports we all know and love). Say hello to the real Korea – we guarantee you'll find a new obsession in these pages.

KOREA IS

SETTING THE SCENE

If you really want to get to know a country, first you need to understand the basics. Located in the easternmost part of Asia, and close to neighbours China and Japan, Korea's geography has long determined its destiny. Throughout a history that dates back some 40,000 years, there have been conflicting kingdoms, multiple invasions, occupation and one devastating division. But through all this, Korea has become a powerful country in its own right. Dense with mountains, rivers and islands, the nation also has a rich variety of dialects, traditions and cuisines. And no matter where they live – the countryside, coastal plains or, for most, the cities – Koreans are unified by their rich history, shared tongue and a determination to look forward. It's these building blocks – geography, history and language – that set the scene and begin Korea's story.

(지도 위의 한국)

South Korea on the map

For a rather small country, Korea packs a lot in: bustling cities, rural highlands blanketed in forests and thousands of islands around its coastline.

Lying in the far east of Asia and connected to the Eurasian landmass by way of North Korea, South Korea is predominantly surrounded by water. The mainland is divided into nine main provinces, and each metropolitan city (including Seoul and Busan) are, administratively speaking, their own provinces too. The three seas that surround the peninsula, meanwhile, are dotted with islands – many uninhabited. And while this all results in an incredible array of landscapes – urban, rural and coastal – the 51 million-strong population is mostly concentrated in cities, leaving great swathes of wilderness largely untouched.

The landmass
Mountain ranges of relatively diminutive peaks have helped separate Korea into regions with unique dialects,

cuisines and customs. The main belt – the Taebaeksan Mountain Range – runs along the east coast of both Koreas, unifying, in a way, the politically divided nations. Sub-ranges extend westward from this "backbone", and from the mountains come mighty rivers that help power the country's hydropower plants. The flattest part of Korea, meanwhile, is the fertile southwest, known as the "rice bowl".

Diverse seasons
This varied topography, and Korea's position within Asia, greatly impacts the seasons. The southern part of the peninsula and its islands are subtropical, where it rarely freezes. For the rest of Korea, winters bring chilly winds from Siberia, and hot summers capped with a rainy season are bookended by pleasant springs and autumns.

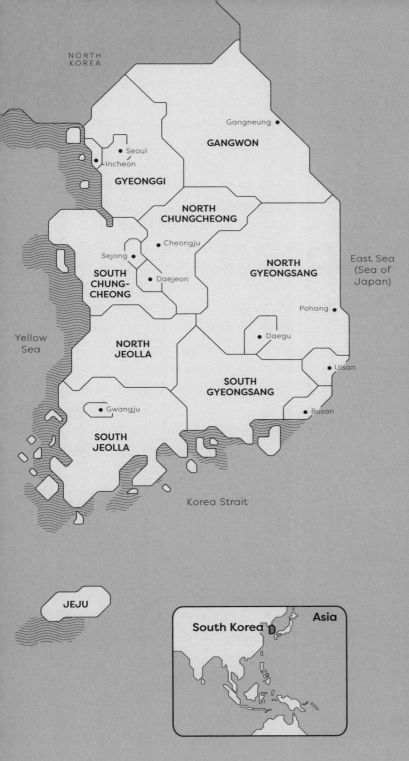

NORTH KOREA

Gangneung •

GANGWON

• Seoul
Incheon

GYEONGGI

NORTH CHUNGCHEONG

• Cheongju

Sejong •

NORTH GYEONGSANG

East Sea (Sea of Japan)

SOUTH CHUNG-CHEONG

• Daejeon

Pohang •

Yellow Sea

• Daegu

NORTH JEOLLA

• Ulsan

SOUTH GYEONGSANG

• Gwangju

• Busan

SOUTH JEOLLA

Korea Strait

JEJU

Asia

South Korea

Korea's provinces

Gyeonggi

This northern province is home to the capital, affluent satellite cities and quiet countryside.

Gangwon

Though little populated, this province's natural splendour and beaches draw visitors all year.

North and South Gyeongsang

Strongholds of tradition and history, these provinces are also home to industrial cities.

North and South Jeolla

Known for its rebellious spirit, the fertile Jeolla region has some of the best food in Korea.

North and South Chungcheong

These slow-paced, agricultural provinces are dotted with famous Buddhist temples.

Jeju

Not far from Japan's Nagasaki Prefecture, the "Hawaii of Korea" has its own dialect and a volcanic topography unique in Korea.

Captivating cities

If there's one stat that tells the history of modern South Korea, it's this: six decades ago, 29 per cent of the population lived in urban areas; today, it's 81 per cent.

Contemporary Korea is defined by its incredible cities. They're the engines that power its ever-growing economy, the laboratories that develop its future-defining technology and the incubators that produce its world-conquering pop culture. Of course, any discussion of urban Korea can only start in one place: Seoul.

The soul of Korea

Often, when talking about a trip to the capital, Koreans will say not just that they're going to Seoul, but that they're going *up* to Seoul. That prepositional embellishment isn't done with any other city. It's impossible to overstate just how central Seoul is to everything

that happens in Korea. It's the political, economic and cultural star the rest of the country orbits. It's been the capital for 600 years, and today, the Seoul Capital Area — Seoul, Incheon and Gyeonggi Province — is home to fully half of Korea's population.

The Han River flows through the heart of Seoul, dividing the city in two. Gangbuk, "North of the River", contains the original parts of the city, defined by ancient city walls that wind over four guardian mountains. Within them are royal palaces and narrow alleys lined with traditional homes called *hanok*. Gangnam, "South of the River", is a recent invention, largely developed in the post-Korean War boom years. Though synonymous with wide boulevards, designer boutiques and posh homes, Gangnam is also the site of immigrant neighbourhoods and expanses of the middle-class apartment towers that define Korea's city skylines.

A need for speed

With so many people and so much going on, Seoul operates at a speed that is by turns thrilling and exhausting. Parts of the city can feel more lively at 3am than most cities do at midday, with people still coming and going from restaurants, bars and *noraebang* (singing rooms).

In the 21st century, much of the city's energy has been directed not at build-first, ask-questions-later development (as it was in the 1970s and 80s), but at creating a more liveable metropolis. Projects like the restoration of the formerly paved-over Cheonggyecheon (Cheonggye Stream), the transformation of a former landfill into the riverside Haneul Park and the general renewed appreciation for *hanok* – many of which have been restored and turned into restaurants – have made Seoul, now more than ever, a place one goes up in the world to.

Seoul's slick cityscape
aglow as night falls

1 Incheon's vivid Chinatown

2 Busan's glistening waterfront

3 Ulsan's lush bamboo forest

4 Daegu's urban riverside

5 Art on display at the Gwangju Biennale, 2021

6 Bibimbap, a Jeonju specialty

BEYOND THE CAPITAL

While Seoul may overshadow the rest of the country, plenty of other cities shine a light on Korea's history, modern development and unique regional cultures.

Incheon

Though part of the Seoul Capital Region, this port town has its own unique character, shaped by a long history as the gateway to Korea. The country's opening to the West in the 19th century can be seen in the high number of churches, and Korea's largest Chinatown stands as a testament to immigration from across the Yellow Sea. Yet the ambitious Songdo development – a new smart city built on reclaimed land – shows that Incheon's gaze is fixed not just outwards, but forwards, too.

Busan

Korea's southeast is anchored by Busan, the country's second-largest city, which sprawls across several peninsulas. Busan is an endearing mix of urbane sophistication — with expensive real estate, glamorous beaches and one of Asia's most important film festivals — and rough-around-the-edges port town charm. It's famed for its distinctive dialect.

Ulsan

Up the coast from Busan, Ulsan is modern Korea in microcosm. Once little more than a fishing village, it became the engine of Korea's economic rise following the Korean War, as the site of the world's largest shipyard and one of the globe's biggest oil refineries. With industrial development came toxic levels of pollution, but since 2004 Ulsan has made huge efforts to clean up. The city's Taehwagang – once nicknamed "the River of Death" – is a prime example, lined with parks and bamboo groves visited by migrating herons.

Daegu

Known as a conservative stronghold (four conservative presidents had their roots here) and the place where Samsung was founded as a business trading in groceries, Daegu is today home to a large student population. As a consequence of its geographic position in a basin surrounded by mountains, the city experiences muggy summers and frigid winters.

Gwangju

Korea's southwest is the southeast's opposite: liberal and agricultural. Gwangju, the southwest's largest city, was the scene of the 1980 Gwangju Uprising, when pro-democracy demonstrators wrested control of the city from the military. The uprising was brutally put down, but it lit a spark that led to Korea's democratization. Gwangju still takes pride in its rebellious history, but today it's known equally for its modern art scene.

Jeonju

North of Gwangju, Jeonju sits amid fertile plains that make up Korea's rice bowl. For centuries, it's been at the centre of Korean cuisine, famed for its bibimbap and *makgeolli*. History is also on full display here in a way it's not in many other Korean cities. For starters, Jeonju has one of the country's best-preserved *hanok* neighbourhoods and most vibrant *pansori* (lyrical storytelling) traditions.

15

Rural living

Rural Korea can often feel like the forgotten Korea, lost in the glare of brightly lit cities. Yet much of Korean culture — cuisine, proverbs, holidays — has its roots in rural lifestyles.

Modern Korea is overwhelmingly urban, but it wasn't that long ago that most Koreans lived rurally. Contemporary Korea's rural areas retain many traces of the nation's past: the pace of life is slower, for one, and much of life revolves around agriculture. Rice paddies and sweet potato farms occupy the plains, and in small towns and villages, traditional markets remain important centres of local commerce.

Folk villages

A distilled version of country life is preserved in Korea's folk villages: rural settlements that exist somewhere between attractions offering performances and programmes to tourists, and genuine repositories of rapidly fading customs. Importantly, they remain living communities, often with residents who can trace their family roots in the village back centuries.

The most famous folk village is Hahoe, outside the city of Andong in Korea's east. Well-kept thatch- and tile-roofed homes cluster on a bend in the Nakdong River, and a patchwork of agricultural fields fills what little land there is between the village and the surrounding mountains. Some 500 years old, it was home to important Joseon scholars and officials. Today, it's typical of a Joseon dynasty clan village, and has even preserved the Hahoe Mask Dance tradition (p156) – a form of entertainment that began as a way to poke fun at Joseon society's rigid social structures.

Preserving tradition

While folk villages curate a representation of the past, contemporary rural life thrives in towns across Korea today. Take the small town of Gongju, the capital of the Baekje dynasty in the 5th and 6th centuries, whose downtown is wedged between the Gongsanseong (Gongsan Fortress)

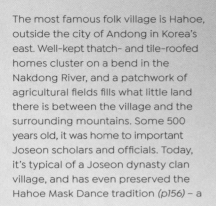

Tile-roofed home in the folk village of Hahoe

and a complex of royal tombs. Past and present bump up against each other seamlessly here – rituals honouring the spirit of a bear from a local myth are still conducted, while hip cafés recall scenes found in Seoul.

In big cities, neighbourhood markets have largely been replaced by department stores; in small towns, they remain a commercial focal point, not least because the older population grew up with them. Jeongseon, a former mining town in Gangwon Province, preserves a uniquely rural Korean tradition: the periodic market. Held on dates ending in 2 and 7, this market sees vendors sell medicinal herbs plucked from surrounding hills.

Perhaps the most noticeable difference from urban Korea is how much older the rural population is, with most young people moving to the cities to study and work. Nevertheless, a few – disenchanted with city life – have opted to pursue *kwichon* (the return to rural life) and have a go at farming, keeping countryside traditions very much alive.

가을 타다
Gaeul tada

To get sentimental in the autumn, as the summer's warmth fades and the leaves begin to fall.

Natural splendour

The deeper into the countryside one ventures, the more bucolic Korea becomes, not least within its 22 national parks. Roughly half of these trace the Baekdudaegan Range, a mountain system – traversing North and South Korea – that runs down the east coast before turning inland and separating the Jeolla Provinces and Gyeongsang Provinces.

In the northeast, the dramatic terrain of Seoraksan National Park has been the subject of landscape paintings for centuries. Granite peaks extending above the clouds crowd the East Sea shores, while lower slopes conceal hidden valleys. Its beauty continues to attract people today. At the range's southern terminus is Jirisan National Park, whose name means "the mountain of the odd and wise people". Seekers still come to its temples in search of enlightenment, or to trek its ridge in pursuit of nature's ineffable magic (the crimson glory of Jirisan's fall foliage is renowned). While the past century saw armed conflict and development devastate Korea's wildlife, these mountains remain a haven for elusive creatures such as elk and Asiatic black bears.

West of Jirisan, the rural county of Damyang is hot on the heels

Above Hiking through Seoraksan National Park

Left Gongsan Fortress in Gongju

of Korea's national parks. With its traditional gardens and bamboo groves, it's considered one of Korea's most beautiful regions. During the Joseon era, it was a place of political exile, but the dissident scholars who were sent here found inspiration in the enchanting surroundings, creating a new poetic form, *gasa*, and writing some of the era's most beloved poetry. Today, Korea's mountain streams, rocky peaks and shadowy bamboo groves provide similar joys — inspiration, cherished traditions and respite from the stresses of city life.

Tea time

Nearly every rural town has at least one dish or agricultural product that's an integral part of its identity. In Hadong county, south of Jirisan National Park, it's tea. Hadong's tea was served to Goryeo and Joseon dynasty kings, and there's a long tradition of using *jakseolcha* (medicinal tea) to treat ailments here. Hadong remains home to many teahouses, where visitors sip green tea over views of forested mountains dotted with Buddhist temples.

Tidal flats of
Suncheon Bay

해안선 따라

On the coast

If anywhere helps Korea live up to its "Land of the Morning Calm" moniker, it's the 2,413 km (1,499 miles) of coastline, where the ebb and flow of the tides dictate everyday life.

The Korean Peninsula divides the waters between China and Japan into the Yellow Sea and the East Sea (also known as the Sea of Japan). Korea's coasts are drastically different: while the east is a single smooth curve from the North Korean border to Busan, the west and south seem to drift into the ocean, riddled with scenic bays and islands.

A natural rhythm

Along the coast everything is driven by the elements. Temperate tides and the changing seasons bring routine to the days, with jobs largely based around the food industry and tourism, and homes sitting alongside estuaries and tidal flats. Nowhere is the water's influence on life better seen than along the northern reaches of the east coast. Long, sweeping beaches like Naksan and Gyeongpo are popular holiday spots, while those in Yangyang are the centre of surfing culture. At the opposite end of the coast, industries like shipbuilding have spurred the growth of Ulsan and other key cities.

While large parts of the coastline are highly developed, much of it remains as nature imagined it. The west coast is arguably Korea's most dramatic landscape, a place of geological marvels, immense tides and devilish currents. The receding water reveals hidden sea caves, like those along the Byeonsan Peninsula, a curiosity of columnar jointing and dramatic cliffs topped with bamboo. The south coast, meanwhile, is distinguished by a series of peninsulas that reach into the sea and are the settings for some of Korea's prettiest cities, including Yeosu and Tongyeong.

Favourite beaches

Korea's beaches bring a surge of energy to the mostly calm coast.

Haeundae

Surrounded by bars, restaurants and clubs, Korea's most popular beach in the southern city of Busan is the place to see and be seen.

Jungmun Saekdal

On Jeju's south coast, this beach is framed by black volcanic cliffs and is a popular spot for water sports.

Naksan

This smooth stretch of golden sand in Gangwon Province offers superb sunrises and plenty of great cafés and restaurants.

Daecheon

The site of the famed Boryeong Mud Festival, Daecheon is the west coast's largest beach at 3.5 km (2.7 miles) long and 100 m (328 ft) wide.

Ingu

On the east coast, this laid-back beach is where young Koreans surf by day and barbecue by night.

Above Haeundae beach in Busan

Right Trading at a wet market at Jeju City, on Jeju Island

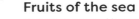

Fruits of the sea

As well as natural beauty, Korea's coastal waters provide the country with a major source of food. Fishing has always had an important place in the east coast's economy, with the waters here supplying squid, mackerel and crabs – staples of the Korean diet. Today, boats come to port in places like Pohang, where wet markets sell the day's catch alongside *mulhoe*, a cold soup made with whatever spare bits of fish are lying around. Along many parts of the west coast, low tide exposes vast mudflats, enabling people who live near the shore to don rubber boots and harvest the clams and *gamtae* (a wispy type of seaweed) that the ocean leaves behind.

In the south, warm temperatures and sea breezes create a bountiful agricultural region. Haenam's cabbage and sweet potatoes,

Goheung's golden *yuja* (yuzu), Namhae's bracken and Boseong's famed green tea — all essential elements of Korean cuisine — are regarded as the country's best. This bounty even extends offshore, with strong, cold, nutrient-rich currents supporting Busan's kelp farms.

Korea's islands

Offshore, Korea has well over 3,000 islands. Warm temperatures, gorgeous scenery and a pair of national parks make the southern islands – of which there seem to be too many to count – popular places to spend a holiday. The largest and most populous island, Jeju, lies 83 km (52 miles) off the south coast, with Hallasan volcano sitting at its very centre. Unsurprisingly, Jeju has always been slightly removed from the rest of Korea, with its own culture and dialect. Once agrarian,

Jeju has increasingly become an international tourist draw, with trendy restaurants and major resorts changing its face. It is, however, primarily a residential place and the only area of Korea where *haenyeo* (p24) still make a living. Of the south's numerous other islands, another of note is tiny Oedo, the entirety of which has been turned into a Mediterranean-style garden.

While the west and south coasts have seemingly too many islands to count, the east coast is sparse. The remote outpost of Ulleungdo is a highlight, and is home to roughly 10,000 people, many living in small fishing villages; at night, the lights of squid boats can be seen from shore. For most, Korea's islands are a break from everyday life – places to honey-moon or spend days surfing. Yet, for many, they're everyday life itself, where time is set to a tidal rhythm.

제주 해녀

Haenyeo of Jeju

Along Jeju Island's volcanic shores, a hypnotic whistling cuts across the waves. These melodic sounds, known as *sumbisori*, form part of the ancient breathing technique used by *haenyeo*, Jeju's unique clan of female free divers, who go deep underwater to harvest marine life. Unaided by oxygen tanks and clad only in wetsuits, face masks and flippers, these divers let out a *sumbisori* after holding their breath for every dive, often 10 m (33 ft) deep.

One of the only examples of a matriarchal structure in Korea, these "Mothers of the Sea" have been the anchor of Jeju since the 17th century. With men dying at war or while fishing at sea, women became the primary bread-winners, and thousands took up the profession.

It's a tough career. Weather permitting, *haenyeo* – many aged over 60 years old, and some in their 80s – harvest up to seven hours a day, 90 days of the year. They straddle a world between life and death daily (prayers are often said before every dive for safety and an abundant catch), but it's a vocation that's built into society. Young girls begin diving with their mothers and grandmothers from about eight years old, learning the breathing technique that's been passed on for centuries. While modern fishing methods and varied career paths have seen the number of *haenyeo* lessen today, the vocation was added to the UNESCO List of Intangible Cultural Heritage in 2016, and remains a symbol of Jeju's utterly unique identity.

Carrying a bountiful catch after a morning dive

(간략한 역사)

A brief history

Long known as the Hermit Kingdom, Korea has been quietly developing over time, absorbing outside influences and responding with world-changing innovations of its own.

Korean early history is a complex story of migrating nomadic tribes and clashing kingdoms. Humans arrived in what is now known as Korea from Siberia about 40,000 years ago, and the earliest kingdom, Gojoseon, is said to have been founded in 2333 BCE. Gojoseon (geographically close to Liaoning Province in China) fostered its own system of rule until 194 BCE, when it was overthrown by former Chinese military leader Wi Man. Wi Man took

advantage of the proximity to China by expanding Gojoseon's territory, leading China's Han dynasty to attack.

Despite initially resisting the Han's attack, Gojoseon collapsed in 108 BCE, and it wasn't long before three new kingdoms arose. The largest, Goguryeo (37 BCE–668 CE), used military prowess to expand until its land stretched north into what was then Manchuria and south into modern-day Gangwon Province; it was through Goguryeo that Confucianism and Buddhism arrived from China. In the southwest arose Baekje (18 BCE–660 CE), a sophisticated kingdom that drew inspiration from China. The third great kingdom, Silla (57 BCE–935 CE), occupied the southeast, with Gyeongju as its capital. Tired of attacks by adjacent kingdoms, Silla made diplomatic overtures

Above Haedong Yonggungsa in Busan, built during the Goryeo dynasty

Left Wall painting from a Goguryeo tomb

to Tang dynasty China (who were exerting a strong influence on the peninsula through religion and the arts) and cemented an alliance. Through this, Silla was able to conquer the Baekje and Goguryeo kingdoms. This alliance wasn't without its problems, as the Tang sought to create colonies on the peninsula. After fighting for years to drive out Tang troops, Silla finally unified the peninsula in 676.

Silla succumbs

Lasting until 935, the Unified Silla period was a golden age, with cultural exchanges established along the Silk Road and through East Asian trade routes. Towards the end of the 8th century, however, power struggles and uprisings saw Silla's authority diminish. While breakaway states

were forming, military commander Wang Geon gained recognition for his campaigns and public generosity; by 913, he was appointed Prime Minister of Taebong state, and managed to gain control (with the help of four generals) over almost the entire peninsula by 918. For his domain, Wang Geon chose the name Goryeo, a nod to Goguryeo. Explorer and writer Marco Polo brought word of this kingdom to Europe, which came to be known in English as "Korea".

In 1231, the Mongols invaded Goryeo. The royal court was moved to the island of Ganghwado, and the general populace fled to islands and fortresses. While resistance was dampened and the country became a vassal state, Goryeo regained autonomy in the mid-14th century,

Above Golden crown from the Silla period

Below King Taejo, founder of the Joseon kingdom

Joseon era inventions

The reign of Joseon's scholar king, Sejong the Great, was a high-water mark for Korean science and technology.

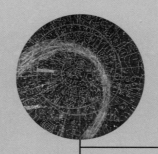

1395

The world's second-oldest surviving astronomical chart, showing 1,467 stars, is commissioned.

1429

Korea's first book on agricultural techniques, called *Nongsajikseol*, is written.

1434

The water clock Borugak Jagyeongnu is built; it signals the hour with musical instruments.

1433

Korean medicine is furthered by the publication of the medical treatise *Hyangyakjipseongbang*.

1437

Several sundials, including a "dangling bead sundial" and "cauldron sundial", are invented.

1442

A rain gauge, *cheugugi*, is designed, making it possible to predict potential harvest sizes.

1448

Singijeon – a bow-and-arrow device that shoots off dozens of arrows at a time – is created.

1447

The Jeongganbo system of musical notation for recording rhythm and pitch is devised.

1443

King Sejong leads the creation of an alphabet, now known as *Hangeul*, for the Korean language.

slowly recovering territory. Goryeo officially came to an end in 1392, when its general Lee Seong-gye defied orders to attack Ming China and staged a *coup d'état*. Known thereafter as King Taejo, Lee named the new kingdom Joseon and moved the capital to Seoul, laying the groundwork for a new era.

Korea's last dynasty

Joseon was Korea's longest dynasty (1392–1910), and adhered strongly to the Confucian ideology *(p42)* that still permeates Korea today. Modern Korea took shape during this era, with many developments led by the respected King Sejong the Great (1397–1450).

In 1590, a newly unified Japan, under the rule of military leader Toyotomi Hideyoshi, sought to expand. Korea – thought to be easy to conquer by virtue of its size and proximity – was a prime target, and in 1592 Japan invaded, starting the Imjin War (1592–1598) and prompting a centuries-long struggle between Korea and Japan. By the time Joseon finally rebuffed the Japanese, hundreds of thousands of its civilians and soldiers had died.

For a short period, Joseon became inward-looking and remained closed to the West, earning it the nickname the "Hermit Kingdom". Its demise began in 1862, when the kingdom was weakened by squabbling factions and peasant revolts that led to the Donghak movement. The Japanese (a constant adversary through the

A new religion

Among Joseon's perceived threats was Catholicism, which entered Korea in the late 18th century through Koreans returning from China. It was seen as incompatible with neo-Confucianism and as a potential disrupter of Joseon's strict social hierarchy, and up to 10,000 Korean Catholics were executed by the authorities for their beliefs. Despite persecutions, Catholicism survived and was officially accepted in 1886.

years) sent thousands of soldiers during this time, using the Donghak crisis as pretext for a takeover.

Japanese annexation

Towards the end of the 19th century, Joseon struggled to respond to a changing world and shifting balances of power. A "shrimp among whales", it was a pawn in other countries' games, and the Japanese invasion kickstarted two big wars over Korea: the Sino-Japanese War (1894–1895) and the Russo-Japanese War (1904–1905). Japan came out on top, officially ending the Joseon dynasty (which had been rebranded the Korean Empire for its last 13 years) in 1910.

The Japanese colonial period was a bitter era for Koreans. Japan exploited the people and resources while stifling Korean identity. Attempts to fight for the country's independence were quashed, especially during the March 1st Movement of

1919 – demonstrations that saw the nation's largest outpouring of discontent during these times.

Things were made even worse by war. Further attempts to suppress the nation's identity and religious expression occurred during World War II: Koreans had to take on Japanese names and worship at Shinto shrines, and thousands of women were forced into sexual enslavement.

Hard times ahead

In 1945, Japan surrendered and World War II came to an end. After 35 years as a Japanese colony, Korea was liberated, but was left with a political vacuum. A trusteeship agreement was reached under which the northern half was to be occupied by the Soviet Union and the south by the US. This division – first made using a straight line, the 39th parallel north – led to the creation of the Democratic People's Republic of Korea (North) and the Republic of Korea (South). In 1953, a restricted area, the Demilitarized Zone (DMZ), was established.

By 1948, North Korea was led by former anti-Japanese guerrilla Kim Il-sung, and South Korea by American-educated Syngman Rhee, who had been active in a government in exile. The North's attempt to invade the capitalist South and create a unified communist country triggered the Korean War (1950–1953). The South was assisted by a coalition of UN Forces led by the US, while the North was backed by Soviet air power and Chinese ground forces. About 635,000 tons of bombs were dropped on North Korea by the US, then the most intensive bombardment of any country.

After the war ended in stalemate, the North and South were among the

1988 Summer Olympics

When Seoul beat Nagoya, Japan, in its bid to host the 1988 Summer Olympics, Korea secured the distinction of becoming the second Asian country to host the event. The Games were a chance for the country to show off its economic progress and sports muscle, and it did just that, coming in fourth for gold medals.

poorest countries in the world, with much of their populations displaced. In the South, President Rhee's reform policies were slow to take effect, and he had to declare martial law to stay in power. After student protests sent Rhee into exile, General Park Chung-hee was prompted to seize power in a coup. Winning a fair vote in 1963 but later resorting to dictatorial methods, Park sought foreign currency and launched a five-year economic plan.

Economic expansion

With the founding of large corporations called chaebol (p70), which took orders from the government, South Korea (Korea hereafter) was primed for an economic surge. Cheap labour

was needed, and a steady flow of country folk gravitated to the major cities. Urban life under Park was tightly regimented, though, and the Korean Central Intelligence Agency (KCIA) ensured that dissent was nipped in the bud. When Park was assassinated by the head of the KCIA in 1979, the nation was stunned.

Succeeding Park was dictator Chun Doo-hwan, whose brutal response to the 1980 Gwangju Uprising stirred popular discontent. While Korea was preparing for the 1988 Summer Olympics, huge protests were underway, with some people demanding democracy and for US troops to leave. Forced to concede, Chun allowed an election to go ahead. When the vote was

held in 1987, the longtime activists Kim Young-sam and Kim Dae-jung both insisted on running. They split the vote, gifting the presidency to Chun's associate Roh Tae-woo, which saw military strongmen dominate politics for a few more years. The two Kims were eventually elected, serving back to back from 1993 to 2003 and changing the political landscape dramatically.

Cultural dominance

In 1997, Korea found itself in trouble. Excessive borrowing by large Korean corporations and banks pushed the country into the Asian financial crisis, with several dozen chaebol forced to declare bankruptcy, leading to bailout packages. Yet, surprisingly, this crisis resulted in the rise of Korea as a cultural influence, spurred on by strong efforts by the Ministry of Culture to beef up the country's

cultural offerings. Hallyu (the Korean Wave), as the movement came to be known, started in the late 1990s and quickly began to earn Korea soft power. This remarkable culture boom – which has since seen K-pop and K-drama reach dizzying heights globally – has made the nation irresistible to cultural consumers. More importantly, it enabled a country without political clout for so long to secure a place on the world stage. Millions of fans have increased tourist numbers drastically, and Korea's reputation has brightened. Meanwhile, Korean cultural products have become so alluring in North Korea – a modern-day Hermit Kingdom – that they've had to be outlawed there.

Future directions

While Hallyu has been a force of great good for Korea's global image, that's not to say that problems don't persist. Gender equality in the workplace is a work in progress, and Koreans' bloated household debt and low fertility rates are cause for concern. Yet, history shows that the nation comes together to meet a crisis. Having been dragged into the power plays of China, Japan, the US and Russia for the past 100 years, Korea has success-fully managed to climb into a league of its own through the cultivation of soft power, technological innovation and an unbreakable determination.

Bong Joon-ho with two Oscars for his film *Parasite*, in 2020

North and South conflict

For over 70 years, North and South Korea have remained locked in a stare-down, with a peace treaty remaining unlikely.

1950

Under Kim Il-sung, North Korea launches a surprise attack on the South, starting the Korean War.

1953

An armistice agreement is signed, fixing the DMZ as the border between the two Koreas.

1976

The Panmunjeom axe murder incident occurs in the DMZ; two US officers are killed by North Korean soldiers.

1968

North Korean commandos nearly succeed in killing South Korean president Park Chung-hee.

1978

South Korean movie director Shin Sang-ok and actress Choi Eun-hee are kidnapped by North Korea.

2006

North Korea holds its first nuclear test, with the goal of developing nuclear weapons.

2019

Kim Jong-un meets US President Donald Trump at the Demilitarized Zone; talks are unsuccessful.

2017

Kim Jong-nam, half-brother of third-generation North Korean leader Kim Jong-un, is assassinated in Malaysia.

2010

North Korean artillery bombards Yeonpyeong Island in South Korea; four are killed.

The Korean language

Spoken by over 80 million people worldwide, Korean is one of the fastest-growing languages on the planet today, undeniably fuelled by the explosion of K-culture across the globe.

Most commonly known as *hangugeo,* the Korean language has long been the official language of both South and North Korea. Today, it's spoken by around 50 million people in the South and nearly 25 million in the North, albeit with some vocabulary and accent variations between the two countries.

Tracing the origins

The Korean language far predates the creation of the writing system, known today in the South as *Hangeul.* Korean is thought to be linked to the Altaic family of languages, which includes Turkish, Mongolian and the Tungusic languages of Siberia. Old Korean, which borrowed Chinese characters to denote Korean sounds, is among the earliest forms of the language, believed to have been used in the Silla period. Middle Korean, derived from Old Korean,

was used from the 10th century, until the end of the 16th century.

Classical Chinese might have been the country's traditional writing system for centuries, but it was complex, and limited to those with access to high education – notably scholars. To tackle the country's illiteracy and make education possible for all, King Sejong initiated a language reform in the 1440s, leading to a new writing system for the Korean tongue. Originally known as *Hunminjeongeum,* this official system was renamed *Hangeul* in the early 20th century.

Building blocks of speech

Today, the Korean alphabet consists of 24 basic letters – 14 consonants and 10 vowels. Some Korean letter sounds

Neon *Hangeul* signs denoting shops and entertainment venues in Seoul

simply do not have English language equivalents, so pronouncing certain words can be tough for English speakers. One Korean consonant, for example, sounds halfway between the English "l" and "r" sounds. The sounds closest to the English letters g, d and b are often phonetically written as k, t and p respectively, and pronounced halfway towards their Roman letter equivalents.

While the building blocks of the language are the same across Korea, there are varying regional dialects and accents (known as *saturi*). One of the most distinct dialects is Jejueo (or Jejumal), found on Jeju island, which uses mostly the same letters as *Hangeul* but also has words that

Konglish

Some of the Korean vocabulary is made up of Konglish: words formed from borrowed English words, commonly known as loanwords. For example, *aisyoping* (eye shopping) is the equivalent of "window shopping", and *haendeupon* (hand phone) is the term for a mobile phone. Many trace the origins of Konglish back to the end of Japanese rule, when the arrival of American soldiers in the South had a huge impact on the Korean language and saw English naturally start to blend with Korean.

Above Statue of King Sejong, the founder of *Hangeul*, in Seoul

Right Calligraphist Yeo Tae-myeong at work

are different from standard Korean. Dating back to the Goryeo dynasty, Jejueo is considered an endangered language by UNESCO, spoken by no more than 10,000 people on the island today.

In the everyday

The teachings of Confucius *(p42)* often infiltrate speech. Respect and honour for others – two key values of Korean culture and Confucianism – are integral to the Korean language. Therefore, different honorifics (terms that express respect) are used in speech depending on the speaker and the listener. Broadly speaking, Korean speech can be split into two styles: *jondaenmal* and *banmal*. *Jondaenmal* is the polite form of speech, used when addressing those older in age and strangers

(even if they're younger). *Banmal* is the casual form of speech, used when speaking to those who are younger, peers and others of close relation. In short: *jondaenmal* is used when stopping someone to ask for directions, and *banmal* is used when having a drink with close friends.

Within the *jondaenmal* and *banmal* styles, there are several speech levels, each with varying degrees of formality and politeness. These are indicated by different verb endings. In the *jondaenmal* style, for the verb *hada* ("to do"), *hasipsio* ("please do it") is one of the most formal ways of telling someone to do something; it might be used on a library sign that says *joyonghi haejusipsio* ("be quiet"). *Haseyo* (which also means "please do it" and comes under the *jondaenmal* style) is less formal, used to address colleagues.

In addition, various honorific titles – such as *ssi* or *nim* – are used after a name or title as part of the *jondaenmal* style. *Ssi* is usually added to the end of a first name to show respect for a person, while *nim* is attached after an occupation (such as *seonsaengnim*, for "teacher") or family member title (such as *abeonim*, for "father").

Learning the language

For the non-native speakers dedicated to learning the language, Korean is the gateway to understanding a K-pop tune or watching the latest K-drama without the subtitles. In 82 countries around the world, more than 200 state-funded King Sejong Korean language education institutes help to make this a reality – testament to the popularity of Korea and its cultural exports.

Korean alphabet

Consonants

Consonants are relatively easy to pronounce. Some consonants are pronounced differently depending upon whether they start or finish a syllable.

ㄱ	ㅂ	ㅋ
gi-yeok	bi-eub	ki-euk
ㄴ	ㅅ	ㅌ
ni-eun	si-ot	ti-eut
ㄷ	ㅇ	ㅍ
di-geut	i-eung	pi-eup
ㄹ	ㅈ	ㅎ
ri-eul	ji-eut	hi-eut
ㅁ	ㅊ	
mi-eum	chi-eut	

Vowels

Of the vowels, eu is arguably the most challenging to pronounce, as there's no English equivalent sound. To pronounce it, make the "euggh" sound (as if expressing disgust).

ㅏ	ㅗ	―
a	o	eu
ㅑ	ㅛ	ㅣ
ya	yo	i
ㅓ	ㅜ	
eo	u	
ㅕ	ㅠ	
yeo	yu	

서예

Calligraphy

The process of producing decorative handwriting with a brush, paper, ink and inkstone, calligraphy is art. The form likely arrived in Korea from China in the 4th century BCE, and writers used the only written medium at the time in Korea: Hanja, a system of Chinese characters. In 1446, calligraphy encompassed a new alphabet, *Hunminjeongeum*, named after a document that detailed how to script every Korean character. Today, this script is known as *Hangeul*.

Many calligraphy styles that later developed – from the standard *panbonche* ("old style") to the elegant *gungche* ("palace style") – tended to mix *Hangeul* with Chinese characters. Pride in the native script began to blossom in the early 20th century, however, with Koreans eager to find self-expression while under Japanese rule. A dominant style of *Hangeul* calligraphy consisted of neatly aligned characters with precise spacing between each one. It wasn't only about what was written, but how, and calligraphy became an art form.

Whether using Hanja (still practiced today) or *Hangeul*, many Korean calligraphers aim for a rough yet harmonious style, freedom within perfection. Calligraphers have crafted their own styles, be it a focus on inconsistent thickness or more playful strokes. Though digitization has taken the wind out of Korean calligraphy, which is rarely taught anymore, it still makes regular appearances across the country, be it graffitied on cliffs or drawn on alcohol labels.

Getting creative at a calligraphy writing event

KOREA IS
UPHOLDING TRADITION

When it comes to the core principles of Korean society, all roads lead to Confucianism. The very heart of Korean tradition, this ancient code of conduct imbues nearly every aspect of Korean culture and society. Dining with friends, family and colleagues? Waiting for the most senior person at the table to eat first is a sign of respect for hierarchy. Exhausted from working overtime and just want to go home? You're still expected to attend after-work company dinners, and show your team spirit. A young man aged between 18 and 28? Expect to enter the military and serve your nation, which comes before everything. While modern lifestyles continue to bring change to the country as the decades roll on, Confucianism still manages to permeate every corner of society – from the world of education to family set-ups.

유교적 사고방식

The Confucian mindset

One of the first things to understand about Korean culture is the emphasis on the Confucian values system, which shapes practically every type of behaviour and social interaction.

It's long been debated whether Confucianism is a religion or a system of ethics, but one thing is clear: this school of thought is the backbone of Korea. Originating from the teachings of Confucius in ancient China, Confucianism is all about promoting a harmonious society; to achieve this, there are certain rules of behaviour and values that people should follow. The building blocks of Confucianism are many, but those that have had the most impact on society are a respect for hierarchy, the emphasis on the group over the individual and the devotion to self-improvement.

Shaping society

A respect for hierarchy is often achieved by recognizing society's superiors, whether they're older in age or rank higher in social standing. As the teachings go, harmony is achieved by behaving a certain way in the five basic human relationships, for example between parent and child. It's the reason why students bow to their teachers, workers stay in the office as late as their boss and children have an unpayable debt to their parents, expected to honour and care for them throughout life.

Adhering to these ranking systems has a profound impact on society at large, where the group is regarded as more important than the individual. Behaving in the interest of the family or the community – by marrying the person that will lift a family's

Above Ceremony honouring Confucius at Sungkyunkwan University, Seoul

Left Neo-Confucian thinker Yi Hwang (1501-1570), who graces the 1,000 won banknote

social status, or choosing a career that supports the nation – is how social order is achieved.

It might, then, seem contradictory that education and striving to better oneself – a very individualistic notion – is so fundamental to Confucianism. Yet, competing against others to get the best grades and win the best job is the way to reach the top of society's hierarchy, where so many want to be.

A lasting legacy

People might not label themselves Confucian today, but the teachings of this centuries-old system have become ingrained in the minds of Koreans. They continue to infuse the pillars of society, including the family, the schooling system, the workplace and the military.

The rise of the system

The first school

The teachings of Confucius arrived on the Korean Peninsula sometime before 372 CE, when the first Confucian academy was founded.

Impact on government

Confucian ideology became entrenched in governance during the Goryeo period (918-1392), because its rules of hierarchy were thought to be suited to bureaucracy.

Overtaking Buddhism

During the Joseon era (1392-1910), politics and society became more Confucian. Buddhism was shunted aside by royalty, who worked to wrest power from monasteries by seizing their land.

Neo-Confucianism

In Confucianism's Joseon heyday, the focus was on neo-Confucianism: a reinterpretation of foundational Confucian ideas that added a spiritual dimension.

Religious beliefs

While Confucianism is a deep-rooted part of daily life, religion is a personal choice for many. Multiple faiths coexist harmoniously here, amid a general spirit of open-mindedness.

With its astounding number of temples and churches, Korea seems like an overtly religious country. And its believers are dedicated: church-goers are ardent, and lay Buddhists regularly do prostrations before Buddha statues. There has, however, been a decline in beliefs, especially among younger Koreans – just under half the population identify with a religion.

Core belief systems

Of the main religions that people practise in Korea, only shamanism is Indigenous. Buddhism, Christianity

and Islam came from abroad but were embraced and refashioned – something that Koreans have done time and again with foreign influences.

Seon (Zen) dominates the many schools of Korean Buddhism. The goal is to achieve a sudden awakening instead of gradually reaching enlightenment over many lifetimes. Among those who take the Bodhisattva vow, giving up all ties and possessions, are monks *(seunim)* and nuns *(biguni)*.

Existing harmoniously with Buddhism is shamanism – the belief that humans can communicate with spirits. Korea is home to hundreds of thousands of shamans, mostly female; a person may become a shaman hereditarily or by being possessed by a spirit. Both types perform *gut*: rituals held for reasons like bringing good luck or exorcizing an evil spirit.

Korean Christianity, meanwhile, is almost two religions. The differences go beyond doctrine and ritual, with Protestant churches often having a veneer of prestige and a business orientation, and Catholicism respected for supporting human rights and democracy. Christianity has also developed beyond the mainstream, with pseudo-Christian cults arising.

Muslims represent just 0.4 per cent of the population. First introduced over 1,000 years ago by Silk Road traders, Islam was bolstered by Turkish soldiers serving during the Korean War. Then, after chaebol (p70) took on projects in the Middle East, some workers returned as Muslim

converts. The first mosque in Korea, and the headquarters of the Korean Muslim Federation today, is Seoul Central Masjid.

Reaching harmony

For the country at large, religion is at its most noticeable during festivals, when even non-religious folk visit temples on Buddha's Birthday or attend church services at Christmas. It's a testament to a well-built society that these multifaceted belief systems coexist together peacefully.

Above Myeongdong Cathedral, a place of worship for Catholics in Seoul

Left Celebrating the Buddha's Birthday at Seoul's Jogye Temple

Cheondogyo

One of Korea's smaller religions, Cheondogyo was founded in the 1860s. Tied up with peasant rebellions, it was created as a reaction against Catholicism, and brings together elements of shamanism, Taoism, Buddhism and Confucianism. This joining together and adapting of multiple religious beliefs makes it arguably the most quintessentially Korean religion of all.

Football fans coming
together for a match

Group dynamics

There's a Korean saying that goes "you'll live if you stick together, die if you're separated". And it's a saying that sums up just how vital the group is to Korean culture.

Korea's emphasis on the collective and the group mentality is – like much of culture – largely the result of Confucianism. Under Confucian teachings, social harmony or order is best achieved when people behave in the interest of the group over their own. This means following specific behaviours and rules, like using an honorific language system that recognizes the social status and age gap between speaker and subject, and adjusting actions in the company of seniors.

Those who deviate from such accepted norms are more often than not seen as disruptors who have upset the group dynamic. In the office, presence at team lunches and after-work dinners is understood to be mandatory; at home, families are expected to adhere to the natural hierarchy between parents, children and elders.

Speaking volumes

Often, words speak louder than actions. In conversation, the pronoun "my" is frequently replaced with its plural form, "our". When referring to one's mother, for instance, a person will call them "our mother" – a way of reinforcing a shared sense of belonging and building solidarity with others. This aversion to using words like "my", "mine" and "I" is one of the most basic expressions of Korea's collectivist culture.

That's not to say that individualism is absent. The country might come together in incredible unity during a crisis or sporting event, but infighting and rivalry are ever-present, too. If the good of the group relies on hierarchies, the competitive drive to rank the highest – becoming a military leader, for example – is by its very nature individualistic. After all, one's place within the group often matters just as much as the group itself.

Collective emotions

Korea is often thought to have a collective psyche, aided by specific emotions that create social bonds.

Han

In the 20th century, *han* – a form of grief or resentment – was a key element of the Korean identity, a powerful emotion that helped make sense of Korea's collective trauma.

Jeong

This shared sense of love, attachment and longing can be applied to people, places and objects. A way to understand *jeong* is to think of the emotion that arises after finding a loved childhood toy.

Nunchi

The ability to accurately assess the mood or ambience of a room and adjust behaviour accordingly, *nunchi* is valued in the workplace and in interpersonal relationships. Those with "quick" *nunchi* are sensitive to body language, speech tone and choice of words.

(나이: 단지 숫자에 불과한가?)

Age: just a number?

"How old are you?" might be a simple question, but in Korea, whether or not you reveal your age depends on both setting and intention. What's more, the answer dictates everything.

Age directly relates to social standing here, and only by knowing someone's age do Koreans know how to address one another. And while disclosing your age might seem like a simple act, in Korea it's not so clear-cut.

So, how old are you?

There are a few things to keep in mind before asking someone's age or disclosing your own. In social environments, where you're trying to create a personal bond with someone, ask the question to determine whether you're the same age, older or younger. The outcome dictates how you proceed. Considering the significance of hierarchy in Confucianism, people are expected to behave according to their standing. For instance, young people must show elders respect such as by using honorifictitles *(p37)* during conversation and bowing. At meals, younger people will distribute the chopsticks,

pour drinks for their elders and wait for the eldest person to begin eating first.

In the workplace, however, it's less common to reveal your age. Instead, people are defined by their roles and inherent hierarchies *(p68)*. In more formal settings, too, it's rude to ask another's age, especially if they're identifiably older. Perhaps nothing has more of an influence on culture than age – it's certainly not just a number.

Calculating age

Revealing one's age was made more complex with Korea's unique calculating system, made up of "Korean age", "international age" and "year age". The "international age" system used around the world sees life start at zero, with an individual's age increasing by a year at every birthday. In "Korean age", Koreans would be considered one year old at birth, with a year added every 1 January. Where "Korean age" came from is a mystery, but it's thought to

Celebrating a baby's official first birthday, *doljanchi*

account for the time in the womb, or to derive from an ancient Asian numerical system in which zero didn't exist. Without calendars or birth records, Koreans might not have known their birth date, and hence marked a year of age at the Lunar New Year.

Many, then, would have a "Korean age" and an "international age", which could be as much as two years apart. For some legal purposes, "year age" is also used, where a baby is born zero and turns a year older every January. The multiple age systems have long posed problems – especially for the military, where males must begin a mandatory 18-month service by the time they turn 28. And these issues are part of the reason why the government announced abolishing "Korean age" in December 2022 in sole favour of "international age" – a move backed by many locals, some of whom will be two years younger when the change comes into effect.

Major life milestones

Baegil
A newborn's 100th day is celebrated with special recognition. It's thought that celebrating the 100th day of life is a response to Korea's previous high infant mortality rate.

Doljanchi
The first birthday involves a huge party. Special food is served and guests dress up.

Seongnyeon-ui Nal
The coming-of-age ceremony in May sees 20-year-olds mark their debut into adulthood.

Hwangap
Reaching the age of 60 is seen as an achievement, largely in response to a time when shorter life expectancies were the norm.

가족 중심의 관계망

Family network

Korea is incredibly family-oriented. Close family units are built upon loyalty, respect and protection of both family members and the family name.

Korean culture begins and ends with family, which is considered a microcosm of society under Confucian philosophy. If good family relations and the hierarchies within them are maintained, and one's family is put before personal desires, harmony and peace will naturally follow.

The family unit

Traditionally, Korean homes have consisted of an extended family – think several siblings, their spouses and children, living in one house with their parents and grandparents. Fathers form the central figure of families in Korea's patriarchal society, while mothers are revered as sacrificial saints and the backbone of the family. A mother is traditionally in charge of managing household finances; when it comes to the older generations, it's not unusual for husbands to have their monthly salaries deposited into an account managed by their wives, who use the funds to cover all household expenses and allocate spending money to their husbands.

Yet, it's safe to say that what was once the norm is no longer the case. Rapid economic growth from around the 1960s and 70s saw many Koreans move away from the countryside to take jobs in larger cities. In the 21st century, people get married and have children later or, indeed, not at all. The multi-generational structure, then, has become less common, and nuclear family models are now the norm. Typical households today tend

Newlyweds wearing
special wedding hanbok

Wedding customs

Proposals

Getting down on one knee to propose isn't the norm; it's not unusual for Koreans to have very short – or no – engagements.

Gifts

Yedan are gifts prepared by the bride for the groom's family, while *yemul* is a gift for the bride from the groom's family. Gifts from both parties may entail luxury goods and food items or cash.

Pyebaek

During this ceremony, the couple wear a wedding hanbok and bow to older members of the family, who speak blessings over them.

Eating noodles

Janchi guksu (banquet noodles) is served at weddings as a symbol of marriage longevity.

Beating the groom's feet

This ritual sees the soles of the groom's feet be hit with a large stick of dried fish, as a way of building his strength.

to see children live with their parents until they're married or move out on their own.

Enduring values

Regardless of this shift, what remains of the traditional family ethos is the utmost respect for parents, elders and ancestors – expressed in direct acts of filial piety. This predominantly stems from the Joseon era, when *yangban* (upper-class men) had to drop everything when a parent died and embark on three years of mourning, where bodily pleasures were forsaken and the mourner lived in a shack beside the grave. While this degree of devotion no longer exists today, there's still an

Above Groom pouring a drink for his bride during a wedding ceremony

Right Placing a crown of good luck on a bride, 20th century

expectation for children (especially the eldest sons) to take care of their parents, financially and otherwise, when they get older.

The traditional role of men and women, based on Confucian teachings, is most clearly demonstrated within the context of marriage. As with the majority of Korean culture, it starts with language, and the Korean words for husband and wife. A wife is known as *anae*, which stems from the words *anjjok* or *anbang* (meaning inside or inside room) and *naebu* (meaning interior). Wives may also be referred to as *jipsaram* (which translates to home person). Meanwhile, a common phrase for husband is *bakkat yangban*, which means an outside nobleman or aristocrat and symbolizes the role of men belonging to the outside world.

Getting married

The decision to get married is certainly not a light one. Traditionally, marriage in Korean society is about more than just two lovers becoming one – it's the joining of two entire family networks. This legacy of families merging has been important for generations, since the family you marry into is believed to influence your life and social standing, for better or for worse.

As such, parents have long been involved in the world of marriage and dating. They know and want what's best for their kids, and desire the next generation to live a better life than they did. A couple intending to

marry usually introduce themselves to each other's families while they're dating, and parental approval for marriage varies. Some parents might desire certain qualities (such as a specific education level, profession or family background) from a potential son-or daughter-in-law, while others may be more relaxed about such things.

As things progress, the two sets of parents are introduced to each other during a meal (known as the *sanggyeonnye*) and the preliminary details of the wedding and married life, like where the couple will live, are discussed. At the start of the Joseon era, women had equal family inheritance rights as men, so it was the norm for husbands to move into their in-laws' household in the hope of gaining a share of their wives'

inheritance. Later in the same period, a new system was put in place that stripped women of their rights to inheritance to further strengthen the established patriarchal social order. Today, it's more common for couples to either live on their own or with the husband's parents after the wedding.

Dating culture

More or less, dating in Korean society is considered a natural precursor to marriage and creating your own family. For some, parents are still involved in the selection of potential suitors for their children through arranged marriages (known as *jungmae gyeolhon*), a matchmaker or a marriage information agency, where they register their child's details. Others may also opt for a *seon* (also known as *matseon*), a slightly formal date typically set up by a matchmaker or through other connections. Though *seon* are held for the prospect of marriage, it doesn't mean both parties must decide to tie the knot after the first meeting. The two might start dating and at some point either get married or go their separate ways.

For others still, however, dating is simply a way to have fun. Being single and unmarried today isn't necessarily

frowned upon or seen as unusual to the extent it may have been decades ago. Many people are focused on their jobs and careers, which see them work longer hours with little or no time for relationships and building a family. For the same reasons, Koreans are getting married later and having fewer children – so much so that the country has the lowest birth rate in the world.

The rise of online dating and apps has contributed to this generational shift (Korea is, after all, home to one of the highest mobile internet connection speeds in the world, p196). And while dating isn't always seen as a means to marriage, many apps still cater to specific

Above Young couple strolling in Seoul

Right Multi-generational family in Seoul, 1990s

requirements, such as certain financial or educational standards. Another favoured way to date is a *sogaeting* – an informal blind date usually set up by friends, which serves as a casual introduction for those looking to date and eventually have a partner.

What's in a name?

Regardless of these changes to the marriage landscape, family will always have a significant place in society. Take the lasting legacy of names. Surnames in Korean culture provide information on a person's background. Nearly half of the Korean population (around 45 per cent) are reported to have one of the three most popular surnames – Kim, Lee or Park (in descending order of popularity) – with around 20 per cent of Korea's nearly 50 million people being a Kim.

So, why is Kim such a common Korean last name? The Kim family clan were the prominent rulers of the ancient Silla kingdom for 700 years. Except for members of the aristocracy or royal class, surnames were a rarity among Koreans for centuries before the Goryeo dynasty, when the king granted surnames to people as a mark of favour. The latter part of the Joseon era saw people adopt family names to help climb the socio-economic ladder, with many choosing the name of illustrious clans such as the Kims. And not all Kims are the same. There are believed to be around 300 or so Kim clans and the lineages

김
Kim

A popular Korean surname, meaning "gold" when written in the Hanja script.

of each are linked to different locations across Korea, such as Gimhae, Gyeongju and Andong.

In official documents and other paperwork, names are always written with the surname followed most commonly by a two-part given name. It's also spoken in the same manner when formally introducing yourself, such as in the workplace or meeting a person for the first time. This specific ordering of the last name before the given name is yet another reflection of the enduring part family plays in a person's identity in Korean culture. Even through the changing dynamics of the 21st century, the strength of the family will continue.

Above *A hanok* in Jeonju Hanok Village

Right Modern apartment buildings in Seoul

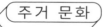
주 거 문 화

At home

The post–Korean War decades reshaped the Korean home, with a huge shift from rural to urban living. Yet, no matter where Koreans live, home is more than a physical structure.

The modern Korean home is often tied up in contradictions. A nice house or an apartment in a posh complex is the ultimate signifier of success to the outside world. Yet the home itself — and particularly the urban home — is a remarkably private place, rarely opened to anyone beyond one's extended family.

Rural vs urban living

In the countryside, home life often resembles what it was in the past. Many people still live in houses with a plot of land and small courtyards, where they might keep some kimchi jars and a *pyeongsang*, a small raised deck where they can relax with neighbours.

Today, however, the average Korean resides in the city. Home is generally an apartment, which might be in one of the skyscraping towers that house Korea's upper-middle and middle class, or an older, less expensive brick building called a "villa". This transition to small apartments in high-density areas has drastically changed how people live. With so many people in such close proximity, noise is a sensitive issue – one of the first things parents buy when their child learns to walk are thick mats for their floors, to spare downstairs neighbours from noisy toddler footsteps. House parties aren't appreciated either; in any case, with bars and restaurants often a short walk away, it's usually more convenient to socialize outside the home.

Inside the home

A key characteristic of Korean home life is how much of it is lived close to the ground. Some people sleep on a mattress on the floor and dine cross-legged at low tables, taking full advantage of their home's *ondol* (p139), an underfloor heating system whose basic design dates back thousands of years. Because of this lifestyle, Koreans are hyper-diligent about keeping the floor clean, and always remove shoes before entering

a home. In fact, every home, no matter the size, will have an area for removing shoes by the front door, often with a built-in shoe closet.

Family space

While family and the home have traditionally been inextricably linked, with three generations often living together, today's most significant housing trend is the rise of single-person homes, which make up one third of all households. One large part of this demographic is young people who are putting off marriage, while another is elderly Koreans whose spouse has passed away. Korea's shrinking population is sure to change home life yet again in the future.

Visiting a home

Koreans rarely visit the home of anyone who isn't a relative, but when they do, certain etiquette is observed. Guests bring a small gift for the host, often something simple and shareable like a cake or bottle of alcohol. For a *jipdeuri* (housewarming party), guests gift toilet paper, symbolizing continuous unspooling of health and success, or detergent, whose bubbles symbolize prosperity. Visitors should avoid dressing too casually; making an effort shows respect for the host.

(성과 성 정체성)

Gender and sexuality

Given the importance that Confucianism places on behaving according to one's rank, it follows that there are strict expectations when it comes to gender roles and sexuality.

Of the five key relationships that Confucianism deems central to society, it's that between husband and wife that defines the role of men and women. According to Confucianism, men (deemed superior) go out to work, while women (deemed subordinate) stay home as caregivers.

During the Joseon era in particular, the three main roles that constituted a "virtuous" woman included being a submissive daughter to her father, wife to her husband and mother to her son. Not only were women expected to be chaste before marriage, they couldn't remarry when their husbands died in order to maintain the purity of the paternal lineage. They were also banned from engaging in direct contact with men (interactions were only allowed with immediate family), and were required to hide their faces in public, forcing them to wear hoods.

Stepping out

Opportunities for women to participate in society began around the late 19th century, when missionaries arrived in Korea and launched schools targeting women's education. The Korean War

marked another turning point; with husbands and sons away at battle, women were forced to support themselves financially. Post-war, they played a crucial part in rebuilding the nation, showing how vital it was to develop their skills, and how self-reliant they could be in challenging situations.

Women's employment increased in the 1960s; since they were paid lower wages, women were often hired for manual jobs. For the first time in a long time, women weren't just mothers or wives, but had their own lives. By around 1963, just under half the female population was contributing to the economy, with numbers growing in the 1970s. Yet, with wages still much lower than men's, the women's movement grew. During the International Women's Year of 1975 and the United Nations Decade for Women (1976–1985), Korean women's groups attended global conferences to highlight the need for better labour conditions and education.

A long time coming

Today, women are active members of the workforce in sectors that span education, medicine, engineering and sports. Perhaps the greatest development has been in education. Among the younger population, male and female students tend to graduate high school at the same rate.

Still, women continue to face an uphill battle, with Korea remaining an ardently patriarchal society. When it comes to gender equality, pay remains a significant issue. Korea has the

Above Women studying for a driving course in the 1960s

Left A married couple in Seoul, 1903

largest gender pay gap among the 38 countries within the OECD (Organisation for Economic Co-operation and Development, an intergovernmental organization), with women earning around a third less than men. Unequal pay is one of many forms of underlying discrimination, despite it being more than half a century since women gained equal constitutional rights.

The impact on sexuality

Such strict ideas on gender have had an inevitable impact on those who don't conform to expected roles and behaviours. Under traditional Confucianism, sex is banned from discussion and considered necessary only to

Marching during the Seoul Queer Culture Festival

bear a child in wedlock. Homo-sexuality is considered taboo and condemned for disrupting the harmony of a society built around a heterosexual family system. As a result, the emergence of LGBTQ+ rights has been slow. It wasn't until the turn of the 21st century that the right not to be discriminated against based on sexual orientation was recognized. A landmark ruling for gender identity came over a decade later in 2013, which allowed transgender individuals to legally change their gender status without undergoing gender reassignment surgery. Freedom is still very limited for the community, though, particularly in the sphere of marriage. Transgender individuals can only get married after their gender has been legally changed, and same-sex marriage is not recognized.

Outside of the law, attitudes within society – especially in the larger cities – are changing. The Seoul Queer Culture Festival has taken place since 2000, and influential K-dramas have raised awareness of the community's struggles by televising strong storylines. The importance of honouring traditional values has long had a stronghold on gender and sexuality, but they're slowly being uprooted and reframed, with younger Koreans leading the way.

Tracing women's rights

The Korean feminist movement has been gaining momentum on the peninsula for over a century.

1886

Ewha Womans University is founded as the nation's first modern educational Institution for Women.

1898

The first Korean women's rights organization, Chanyang-hoe, is founded by wealthy widows.

1991

A revision to Korean family law entitles women to rights after divorce, including a child custody agreement.

1987

The Equal Employment Act is passed to prevent discrimination in hiring and promotions.

1948

Women gain equal constitutional rights to pursue education, work and public life.

2005

The *hoju* system – a family registry where only a male can be listed as the head of a family – is abolished.

2019

Korea's National Assembly is mandated to rewrite laws around abortion and to decriminalize the procedure.

2018

Korea's #MeToo movement is ignited after a female prosecutor claims she was sexually harassed at work.

2013

Korean women's enrolment rate in higher education begins outpacing that of men.

이마
지방이식
헤어라인 교정
모발이식
눈매교정술
안면윤곽
코 재수술
물방울모양 가슴성형
* 이해를 돕기 위한 이미지 사진으로 실제와 다를 수 있습니다.
수술 부위:

SPOTLIGHT ON

이상적인 외모상
Beauty ideals

Though aspirational beauty is not unique to Korea, it's fair to say there's an outsized importance placed on physical appearance here. For women in particular, there's a pressure to meet gendered expectations. Here, skincare shops line city streets and ads for plastic surgery dominate the subway. It's socially acceptable – but not always agreeable – for people to comment openly on each other's weight and looks.

In this competitive society, beauty is capital. Headshots are often attached to job applications, and the more "attractive" candidates often have an advantage. Many people strive to fit Korea's narrow – and Western-influenced – idea of beauty, from pale skin and a V-shaped face for women to a tall nose and lean, muscular body for men. This desire to conform has led to Korea becoming the plastic surgery capital of the world, with the highest number of procedures per capita. Double eyelid surgery is especially common, to make eyes bigger and rounder.

The rise of the global #MeToo movement, however, has empowered some women to revolt against Korea's beauty-obsessed culture. The 2018 "Escape the Corset" campaign saw followers throw out their makeup and chop off their hair. Younger women, meanwhile, have begun to reject thinness and fair skin in favour of *geongangmi* (healthy beauty), an aesthetic that prizes lean muscle and bronzed skin. Surgery ads might dominate, but aspirations are shifting.

Plastic surgery ads at a subway station, Seoul

교육

Educating the nation

Education – and the success that comes from it – is an overriding obsession. Cram schools are rife, the tutoring industry is huge and Korea ranks high on the world's most-educated list.

In this fiercely competitive society, education has always been the way to get ahead in life. And while this focus on personal achievement might seem at odds with Confucianism's emphasis on the group mindset, it's more complex than that. The more educated you are, arguably the more opportunity you have throughout life. And, since Confucianism centres around hierarchy, the majority of people strive to do well in order to rise to a respectable level in society.

A marker of status

How educated a person is has long had a profound impact on family, too. During the Joseon dynasty, *yangban* (nobility) status was not granted by family lineage alone. A key way to achieve power for your family was by passing the *gwageo* (national civil service exam), which required years of studying Confucian teachings. But there was no room for complacency: a family could lose their privilege if four generations failed to pass the exam.

The *gwageo* was discontinued in 1894, but the sheer drive to succeed both for oneself and for one's family has remained.

The school system

Korea now sustains a school system open to all. Japanese colonialism introduced primary and vocational schools, and after World War II, Korea adopted an education system patterned on that of the US. What followed were government reforms and investments to improve access, and make elementary and middle school compulsory. This effort paid off, with the country becoming one of the world's most educated.

Korea's public school system consists of six years of elementary (starting age seven), three of middle and three of high school. The curriculum is set by the Ministry of Education. Core subjects during elementary school include maths and Korean language, as well as morality and English (starting age nine). From middle school onwards, classes are a mix of mandatory subjects like social studies, and electives such as environmental education. Once in high school, students can choose to enter a specialized institution like a computer science school, or a vocational high school for a trade like car repair. A number of private (and expensive) international schools offer an English immersion environment. Speaking English carries prestige and can offer many advantages, and it's common for middle and high school students to study abroad in an English-speaking country for up to two years.

The escalator to success

As is true of so many families, many parents dream of their children entering law or medical

The Suneung

Korea's infamous standardized test isn't just a time of stress for students – it impacts the entire country. Once a year in November, banks, businesses and the stock market open an hour later to ease traffic congestion, and planes are banned from take-offs and landings during the English listening test. Kids running late are also privy to free police escorts to their testing site.

school, or perhaps a reputable a company like Samsung. And a degree from a leading university is usually the only way to achieve such occupations. Korea has over 200 universities, but places at the top institutions are fiercely fought after, including the "SKY" schools — Seoul National University, Korea University and Yonsei University – as well as the Korea Advanced Institute of Science and Technology (KAIST) and Sungkyunkwan University. As such, parents strive to live in areas with good schools – it's thought that even going to a top nursery could eventually lead to a spot in a prestigious university.

Getting into a good university requires a superb grade on the College Scholastic Ability Test (the *Suneung*). To prepare, parents may enroll their children in after-school academies *(hagwon)*, often beginning with English playschool at age 4. To gain an edge, some students take private lessons at home (Korea has one of the world's largest private tutoring industries).

Above A 21st-century re-enactment of the *gwageo* exam

Left High school students learning in Seoul

Many families spend half their income on such expenses – one of the many personal sacrifices to secure the best education for their kids. Things heat up at high school, with students participating in teacher-supervised self-learning sessions that often last until 10pm; cramming then continues at home. This pressure leads to burnout, depression and anxiety, with young Koreans among the world's unhappiest for their age group.

Future of education

It's not all about getting that top job, though. Beyond the school system are numerous other institutions, such as community centres, offering education to the public. Some people are forgoing the prescribed path to become a doctor or a lawyer and are instead pursuing education for pleasure. Computer coding, for one, has become a favourite hobby – little surprise for a country that fosters a huge internet culture.

However, the future of higher education hangs in the balance. Due to Korea's low birth rate, mid- and bottom-tier universities are having trouble keeping some departments running, and many rely on foreign students to bolster enrolment. As a result, Korea will have progressively fewer graduates for the next 20 years.

Working hard

In Korean society, work is life and life is work. Self-sacrifice through hard work is part of the national ethos, with shops staying open late and office employees often working until dawn.

No matter how long the day has been, it's rude to leave work before the boss – a sign of respect for superiors that drives corporate life. The hierarchies of Confucianism, as well as a touch of military organization, permeate the workplace, and everyone must know their place. To the uninitiated, the corporate pecking order can be bewildering, with a wide spectrum of job titles and seniority. But everyone behaves according to their role.

It should be stressed, though, that an office team can feel a lot like

a family. For one, the youngest member is called *mangnae* (the baby of the family). But there's a pressure, in the form of enforced social bonding, that comes with maintaining these familial dynamics. Teams are expected to eat lunch together, and someone who sneaks off for a solitary meal is considered impolite. Indeed, team-building is so important that it sometimes takes precedence over results. When a new hire arrives, much time and effort is devoted to building friendly relations. Even after work, colleagues are expected to attend team dinners *(hoesik)* to bond. While this might be a chance to blow off steam, it also means sacrificing personal time and enduring long hours. The purpose of all this? To cement comradeship and develop a strong family unit that works as one to complete goals and deadlines.

Approach to business

Obligations are slowly changing, though. Work might be the focus of life, but – as it is the case around the world – a job for life is no longer set in stone. Younger generations in particular are shaking up a workforce built around company loyalty, changing employers or fields in quick succession. While many work hard to rise to the top, others are content to try something, do the bare minimum and move on to the next thing.

That's not to say those who don't subscribe to traditional work culture have it easy; going against the grain and not striving for greatness can be seen as letting society down. And despite efforts to strike a better work-life balance, Korea's work culture can be challenging on many levels, and for many people. However, with the practices in place (such as *hoesik*) constantly being reviewed and coming under scrutiny, Korea could see more changes to its work culture in the not too distant future.

충실
Chungsil

Meaning sincerity, being totally dedicated to your company and sacrificing everything for them.

재벌

Chaebol

It cannot be overstated how much power chaebol – business conglomerates, including LG and Samsung – wield in Korea. The word comes from the Chinese for "wealth" and "clique", and it's an apt name: these huge corporations are usually controlled by affluent groups or families with huge influence over national affairs. Yet, missing from this etymology is the scale; as much as 90 per cent of Korea's gross national income comes from chaebol.

After all, they were made to dominate. Many date back to the Japanese colonial period, when they were launched by small business owners with drive (Samsung, for instance, initially operated as a grocery trading store). When President Park Chung-hee outlined a plan in 1961 to build up national industries, chaebol were vital, and thrived through preferential treatment. Largely free of competition and regulation, they benefited Korea by producing cheap export goods – helped, no less, by a huge industrious workforce

It's not easy working for a chaebol. Positions are competitive, and the work can be high-pressured. On top of that, promotions to the top can be hard to come by, with many chaebols seen as dynasties where male founders let their progeny take over. But change is afoot. Take female-run online platform operator Naver, which makes a point of not getting family involved. The future of chaebol offers hope that worker's rights will become more engrained, and that nepotism is a thing of the past.

Samsung's slick global headquarters in Seoul

군사적 전망

A military outlook

Since the Korean War was suspended in 1953, South Korea has had to maintain a state of military readiness, both by hosting US troops and building up a strong army of its own.

When a young Korean man (and it is only men) leaves for his 18 months or more of required military service, he is armed with advice from his parents. Conscription is both a departure from adolescence and a sombre setting aside of personal aspirations for the sake of the nation. Nowhere is rank and hierarchy more apparent than in the military, where joining is an inevitability, as opposed to a choice.

Intensive training

During the Korean War, South Korea struggled against an army that was better equipped and trained – something they've since worked hard to avoid repeating. While some men attend military academies to become career soldiers, most enter the military through conscription, which has been going strong since 1957. The minimum 18-month term of service is completed between age 18 and 28; after the 18 months, one enters the reserves, having to do several days of training a year for the next eight or so years. To minimize career disruption, many opt to finish their service halfway through university.

The potential hardships of military life include basic training, spartan living conditions and exposure to the blistering elements — especially for those stationed near the Demilitarized Zone (DMZ). Still, military service has become easier, with more days off and phones now allowed inside facilities.

A different route

Perhaps preferable to standing sentry each day is a position in the KATUSA program (Korean Augmentation to the United States Army). KATUSA soldiers serve as interpreters and facilitators for the US Army, and need English fluency; the qualified are chosen by lottery. Others are granted exemption from military service for health reasons, and are referred to half-jokingly as "sons of God". Those exempt (including objectors like Jehovah's Witnesses) are given other positions, such as working in a nursing home. Exemptions also go to any man who wins a medal in the Olympics or Asian Games, or who places first in a classical music or ballet competition and thus boosts Korea's image (though they still have to do four weeks of basic military training). Much public debate has circled around whether K-pop stars, like BTS, should be exempt too (eventually, members of the band did have to sign up).

The future of service

In this male industry, women can only join the military voluntarily. One avenue is the Reserved Officer Training Corps (ROTC) programmes at women's universities. With Korea's low birth rate steadily decreasing, however, women may well be forced to sign up in the future – a proposal raised by a lawmaker in 2021 – for the sake of the nation.

The DMZ

When Japan lost World War II, Korea fell into trusteeship: the USSR managed the northern part, and the US oversaw the south, with a straight line drawn across a map of the country to decide the territories. After the Korean War ended in a stalemate, a border was created along the line of ceasefire. Though termed the Demilitarized Zone, the 4 km- (2.5-mile) wide DMZ – today, mostly untouched wilderness – is in fact intensely militarized, filled with landmines and patrolled by soldiers.

KOREA IS
ADDING FLAVOUR

Asking "Have you eaten?" is one of the most common ways to say hello in Korea – and that tells you everything you need to know about food's role in society. Superstition dictates that rice cookers should be one of the first items brought into a new home, and weather reporters guide the public on when to begin preparing kimchi (for which Korean engineers have invented a special fridge for storage). And while you might have heard of the likes of kimchi and bibimbap, there's so much more to Korea's cuisine. Spicy rice cakes dominate street food stalls, comforting seaweed soups mark birthday meals and bottles of soju are staples on nights spent socializing with friends. The best way to get to know Korea is to go out for a meal – and that's easily done in a country where almost every gathering is an excuse to eat out and eat well.

Typical Korean table
setting, complete
with rice, fish, meat
and soup dishes

(대표 음식)

Signature dishes

**It's not just K-pop and K-drama that have
taken the world by storm – vibrant, spicy and
aromatic Korean food has been a key driving
force of Hallyu, and with good reason.**

What makes Korean cuisine so
distinctive – and so popular – is
the irresistible interplay of textures,
temperatures and flavours that can
be had in a single bite. There's the
head-spinning spiciness and garlic-
packed intensity of its most fiery

foods. There's the tang, freshness
and crunch of its flagship fermented
cabbage dish, kimchi – once little
heard of outside of Korea, and
now a staple around the world. In
fact, words like bulgogi, *japchae*,
kimbap and *samgyeopsal* have

become so ubiquitous in the English language, they've entered the Oxford English Dictionary.

The everyday diet

A typical Korean meal involves various dishes: a bowl of rice, a soup, kimchi and banchan, a series of shared side dishes that often includes seasoned vegetables. A protein such as grilled fish or marinated pork might also be served to round out the meal. Table settings are always the same. The bowl of rice is placed on the left, with the soup to the right; a spoon and chopsticks lie to the right of the soup bowl, often on little spoon rests. If the main dish that day is a stew, or *jjigae* (in which case soup is not served), often it will be cooked in an earthenware pot and served straight from the stove to the centre of the table.

Korean meals are not complicated multi-course affairs, and everything is eaten at once. The basic concept is to take a little bit of everything between bites of rice and spoonfuls of soup. No two bites are the same; chopsticks and spoons alternate between the dishes, combining aromas, flavours, textures and temperatures.

A change in tradition

Not every meal, however, follows this classic composition (carbs, vegetables and very few deep-fried foods). Since the 1990s, economic prosperity and Western influences have transformed eating habits. If all meals were once solely Korean foods, Western foods are making more regular appearances. Instead of *doenjang jjigae* for breakfast, people might eat croissants; rather than *kimbap* for lunch, some will tuck into a burger; and in lieu of *jjamppong* for dinner, fried chicken might be served. Dairy has also entered recipes of the last decade, with fast food chains and restaurants topping foods like spicy rice cakes with cascades of oozing, melted mozzarella cheese. Cream, too, is being combined with gochujang (a red chilli paste) to create a Korean–Italian rosé sauce.

Despite this evolution, the Korean palate is conditioned to crave spicy, garlicky, fiery flavours by virtue of the country's culinary repertoire. So, while there's a time and place for fusion recipes, traditional dishes that have long sustained Koreans will always be the heart of food culture.

The original veganism

In the 2020s, English-language influencers gained social media fame for promoting "vegan K-food". But for 1,700 years, monks and nuns have followed a plant-based diet as prescribed by Buddhist philosophy. Where Korean temple food differs from trendy veganism is the exclusion of pungent aromatics like onions, garlic and leeks, believed to distract from spiritual practice.

1 Seasoned Korean
Fried Chicken

2 A vibrant bowl of
beef bibimbap

3 Cooking a stew at
a market in Seoul

4 Bulgogi topped
with mushrooms

Korea excels in too many tasty dishes to count, and can do icy broths just as well as fiery noodles. There are, nonetheless, some specific go-to favourites, either unchanged for centuries or bold and new.

Korean Fried Chicken

Also known as KFC, fried chicken is a relatively modern – and international – addition to Korea's culinary landscape, satiating a generation that desires fast comfort food. It's all about the seasoning that's added, whether it's a garlic, honey and soy sauce or a sweet, spicy and sticky gochujang glaze. While KFC can be eaten as both a full meal or an appetizer, it's most commonly enjoyed on nights out with a beer. In fact, the blending of chicken (*chikin*) and beer (*maekju*) has birthed a whole new word for the occasion: *chimaek*.

Bibimbap

Literally meaning "mixed rice", bibimbap is a prime example of flavour harmony and nutritional balance that makes Korean cuisine so special. The globally loved dish consists of rice topped with an assortment of seasoned vegetables (like spinach, carrots and sprouts), marinated beef, a fried egg and a spoonful of gochujang. Sometimes served in a hot stone bowl, all of the ingredients are meant to be mixed together and eaten with a spoon.

Soups and stews

Rice-based meals are often served with some sort of soup, be it a watery broth-based soup (*guk* or *tang*) or a thicker, heartier stew (*jjigae*). Common *guk* include seaweed (*miyeokguk*), spicy beef (*yukgaejang*) and soybean sprout (*kongnamulguk*); popular *jjigae* include soybean stew and kimchi stew. *Jeongol*, meanwhile, is the Korean version of hot pot: a communal dish of meat, seafood or dumplings, together with broth and vegetables. It's often cooked on a portable gas stove straight on the dining table and eaten as the main meal.

Bulgogi

It might mean "fire meat", but bulgogi isn't spicy. Rather, this dish is made up of thin slices of beef marinated in a sweet soy sesame sauce, often with a touch of garlic. Records indicate that the tradition of roasting marinated meat stretches back to one of the earliest kingdoms, Goguryeo (37 BCE–668 CE), when it was cooked on skewers before the introduction of grills. Later during the Joseon dynasty, the thinly sliced meat was a specialty served at the royal court and enjoyed by the country's elite. Today, the dish isn't reserved for the wealthy, and is commonly cooked at home, be it on a stove-top griddle or barbecue, or stir-fried in a pan.

Tteokbokki

This popular street food dish consists of soft and chewy rice cakes and fish cakes simmered in a sweet and spicy gochujang sauce. Innovative tweaks to the dish range from rosé and carbonara cream sauces to toppings like melted cheese and sausages. The dish also comes in varying degrees of spiciness, with the hottest versions sought out by stressed workers and students, since spicy foods release endorphins.

Samgyeopsal

For this barbecue favourite, thick and fatty slices of pork belly are cooked unseasoned for good reason. The pieces of meat are meant to be eaten in lettuce and perilla leaf wraps, and topped with condiments like sesame oil or *ssamjang* (a pungent, intensely savoury mix of gochujang, or chilli paste, and *doenjang*, or bean paste), as well as slices of raw garlic, pieces of raw hot chilli peppers or fried kimchi. The result is an explosion of flavours, textures and temperatures.

Japchae

This colourful festive dish dates back to the Joseon era, and makes regular appearances as a side dish at special occasions and home parties today. *Japchae* is prepared with cellophane noodles *(dangmyeon)*, an assortment of sautéed vegetables (such as spinach, red peppers, carrots and mushrooms) and seasoned meat, all of which are topped with soy sauce and sesame oil before serving.

Jjajangmyeon and jjamppong

Noodles are a staple ingredient in many beloved dishes. *Jjajangmyeon*, for one, is a Korean-Chinese black bean noodle dish invented by Chinese migrant workers living in Korea in the early 20th century. *Jjamppong*, a spicy seafood noodle soup, is also a Korean-Chinese dish. Both are popular delivery items, and *jjajangmyeon* is traditionally ordered on moving days because it's cheap, cheerful and no-fuss.

Naengmyeon

A summertime staple, *naengmyeon* is actually a North Korean speciality. Chewy, thin buckwheat and potato starch noodles are served in an icy cold broth of beef or radish water kimchi, and topped with sliced cucumbers, beef, boiled egg and pear. The soupless version is topped with a sweet, spicy and sour gochujang sauce and is called *bibim naengmyeon*.

Kimbap

The classic seaweed rice roll, *kimbap* is a standard picnic and lunchtime food. Rice, bulgogi, pickled radish and seasoned vegetables are all rolled up in sheets of laver, which are brushed with a shiny coat of sesame oil before being sliced into rounds. Trendy *kimbap* recipes today include fillings like melted cheese and spicy noodles.

1 A batch of *tteokbokki*

2 Grilling *samgyeopsal*

3 A serving of *japchae*

4 *Jjajangmyeon* topped with an egg

5 *Naengmyeon*, served cold

6 Cylindrical *kimbap* rolls

김치

Kimchi

A warm bowl of rice with kimchi is a meal. A warm bowl of rice with pork, lettuce and soybean-paste soup but no kimchi isn't – not quite. Kimchi is an obligatory part of every meal, whether at home, fast-food joints, army canteens or fine dining establishments. Its combination of spicy, sour, sweet, salty, bitter and umami flavours – together with the tang of fermentation – render it flexible enough to pair with almost any Korean ingredient. And with at least 200 varieties, kimchi is firmly rooted at the centre of Korean cuisine.

It's not just a food, though: it's also a way to measure time. For hundreds of years, families have gathered at the onset of winter for *kimjang*, the practice of preparing enough kimchi to get them through the coming months. Today, *kimjang* might not be a matter of survival, but it remains a major custom. In the run-up to the *kimjang* season, the media updates households on cabbage prices, and weather forecasters prepare reports on the best time to get started.

The best-known type of kimchi, and the focus of *kimjang*, is *baechu* (Napa cabbage). Families set out large plastic tubs of lightly pickled cabbages and seasoning paste in their yard or living room and begin the task of seasoning each cabbage leaf by hand. Every family's recipe is unique, but the mixture generally includes salted seafood, green onion, sticky rice paste, garlic, ginger and red pepper powder. With seasoning complete, the good stuff is stored in a special kimchi refrigerator, ready to eat with every meal.

Preparing kimchi during a festival in Seoul

음식 문화

Food culture

So much more than sustenance, food is a demonstration of the values that shape Korean society, from being in harmony with the land to finding pleasure in the everyday.

Served in dishes refined over generations, with the best seasonal produce used fresh or carefully fermented, Korean cuisine is now globally known for its delicious flavours.

Balancing the body

Historically, Koreans placed huge importance on food as medicine, a concept known as *yaksikdongwon*. When consumed at the right time, food is seen to have powerful restorative properties. To keep illness at bay and maintain equilibrium in the body's *eumyang* (the duelling forces of negative and positive energies known in Chinese as yin and yang), it's vital to eat in harmony with the seasons and the body's needs. In the ancient royal court, this harmony was achieved by preparing a balance of foods in Korea's five cardinal colours, *Obangsaek* *(p143)*: white, black, green, red and yellow.

While this form of preparation is less relevant today, food's healing power is still valued. Take the concept of *iyeolchiyeol*: fighting fire with fire. On the hottest days of the year, Koreans consume a boiling hot chicken soup, *samgyetang*, as a cooling strategy. The premise? Sweating profusely will regulate body temperatures, while the ginseng, garlic and jujube-infused broth will replenish the body with the nutrients it needs.

Above Harvesting fields in Boseong, South Jeolla Province

Left Crocks for storing fermented vegetables

The land's gifts

Korean cooking often works with the seasons. Covering over 70 per cent of Korea, mountains and forests account for a food heritage that's heavy on greens foraged in spring. Miles of varied coastline, meanwhile, yield rich seafoods year-round. One of the defining aspects of Korean cuisine is the use of fermentation to preserve the season's best produce. While the technique was created around the 3rd century as a way to consume meats, fish and vegetables all year, it also supercharges nutritional value and intensifies flavours.

The varied climates, geographies and histories of the nine provinces have yielded distinct cooking styles and regional specialties, from Jeonju's bibimbap to Seoul's hearty ox bone soups. As tastes continually evolve, flavours remain in harmony with the country's diverse landscapes.

Rules for eating

How Koreans eat their food is just as important as what they're eating, and decorum is key.

Go by age

Custom dictates that the most senior person at the table should always eat first.

Speaking before eating

Before tucking in, it's good manners to say *"jal meokkesseumnida"* which translates to "I will enjoy this meal". After the meal, express gratitude by saying *"jal meogeosseumnida"*, or "I ate well".

The rice bowl

It's impolite to bring a bowl of rice to your mouth when eating; it should be left on the table.

Using chopsticks

Chopsticks should never be stuck vertically in the middle of the rice bowl – a gesture used for rites honouring the dead. It's also rude to poke and dig around in shared dishes with chopsticks.

(가정에서의 식사)

Dining at home

As in many cultures, the heart and soul of the Korean home is the kitchen, where flavourful dishes are cooked up and family values shine.

The Korean word for family, *shikgu*, carries another meaning: people who eat together. Family meals at home are communal experiences, especially on occasions such as birthdays or anniversaries, when the table groans under the weight of up to a dozen banchan (side dishes). As busier schedules threaten communal dinners, however, Koreans seek new ways to conserve the sanctity of the table.

From kitchen to table

Traditional Korean cooking has little use for an oven, so many homes don't

have one (if they do, some older folks use it for storage). Cooking is mostly done on hobs or portable gas burners, which are used to re-create the Korean barbecue experience. Almost all households have a kimchi refrigerator, with special sensors to monitor the fermentation process, an air fryer and a rice cooker (an old superstition says when someone moves, their rice cooker should be the first thing they bring into their new home).

Once the cooking is done and the table has been laid (p77), eating commences in a communal way. Family members work their way around the spread of food, plunging their spoons into the same bubbling pot of kimchi stew, taking turns picking the flesh off a pan-fried fish and putting a little bit of everything onto their plate.

A new era

However much importance is placed on upholding these communal dining traditions, the demands of modern life – primarily long working hours – now make home cooking less common, and meals have generally become simpler affairs. Large family dinners are either rushed or reserved for the weekend. As such, it has become less about spending time in the kitchen daily, and more about pragmatic batch cooking, ensuring there are enough leftovers to get the family through the week. It has also become common to grab ready-made banchan from grocery stores, or to fall back on takeaway meals.

The density of city life and proximity to restaurants make delivery services incredibly fast, and a high penetration of mobile phone use and one of the world's fastest internet connections make ordering food particularly efficient. But ordering takeaway doesn't skimp on the "at home" experience – some restaurants deliver food in regular bowls with metal cutlery. When finished, customers collect the plates and leave them outside the door for the delivery person to collect a few hours later.

The rapid growth of single-person households has also changed eating habits. In 2020, the number of single households stood at 6.64 million, up 28 per cent from 2015. Mukbang (eating broadcasts, p197) owe some of their popularity to single-household viewers who treat the mukbangers as their virtual dinner companions.

Though habits at home may be changing, the desire to eat collectively hasn't gone away in Korean society. Increasingly, and perhaps inevitably, dining habits are migrating to the local restaurant, of which there are a remarkable abundance across the country.

Above A traditional Korean kitchen, complete with rustic pots and pans

Left Serving tea with small dishes in a kitchen in Seoul

Socializing at
a barbecue
restaurant in Seoul

KOREA IS
**ADDING
FLAVOUR**

(외식 문화)

Dining out

Eating out is a huge part of food culture in Korea, an obsession that's reflected in Seoul's innumerable restaurants — one of the highest concentrations per capita in the world.

Preparing Korean meals, with their many banchan (side dishes), can be a prolonged process, and the duties of modern life mean it regularly makes more sense to eat out than to cook at home. It helps that many restaurants are affordable and stay open late, and that the food is healthy. In Seoul, fast food joints crowd subway stations, business districts are filled with food spots, and every neighbourhood has streets lined with restaurants. Outside the capital, the smallest village will have options for eating out, too.

Better together

Food is an essential part of any get-together, and restaurants are perhaps Korea's most important social venues: the setting for family gatherings and team-building events with colleagues. With many restaurants specializing in just one or two dishes, the decision of what to eat is usually made as a group. And since most dishes are communal, food is shared. At many restaurants, servings for a single person aren't available.

While ordering and eating may be communal, paying generally isn't. It's common for one person to pick up the entire tab, with the understanding that someone else will get it next time or pay the bar bill later on in the night. Members of the younger generation, however, are increasingly comfortable bucking tradition, often going Dutch or eating by themselves.

A fine approach

In the past, Korean haute cuisine referred to the food served to Joseon royals, utilizing the best ingredients from across the country. More recently, the nation's fine dining was epitomized by *hanjeongsik* (Korean *table d'hôte*), an extravagant version of a basic Korean meal, consisting of rice, soup and an inordinate number of side dishes.

Today, Korea has an established fine dining scene, though it remains concentrated in Seoul, where all of the country's Michelin-starred restaurants are. While foreign offerings like French and Japanese were once seen as the epitome of haute cuisine in Korea, the country's top chefs are seizing on Korean food's global popularity to elevate the cuisine. For some chefs, this means reinterpreting traditional dishes and sourcing their own ingredients.

Meat feasts

When it comes to nights out, little beats a *gogitjip*, or barbecue joint. *Gogitjip* typically serve both beef and pork, and high-end restaurants often advertise Hanwoo: beef from a native breed of cattle, renowned for its fine marbling. Even the most modest *gogitjip* seem to effortlessly achieve the combination of delicious food and genial atmosphere. Guests cook their own meat over charcoal or gas tabletop grills. Accompanying the meat are rice, kimchi, garlic, *ssamjang* (a mix of soybean paste and gochujang) and a handful of other side dishes, giving diners the opportunity to make it according to their taste. The sense of conviviality is heightened by the fact that barbecues are always paired with beer and soju, so every dinner at a *gogitjip* feels like a party.

Street eating

The fastest, easiest and cheapest place to eat out is on the street, where the warm glow and aromatic steam emanating from a street stall is hard to resist. Street food has long had a key place in dining culture; in the impoverished years after the Korean War, it provided cheap but filling meals, and it remains a reliable staple of students, low-wage workers and solo diners. Street food can be found just about anywhere people might want an impulsive

Above Eating at a stall at Gwangjang Market, Seoul

Left Haute cuisine, beautifully presented

snack. Little stands sell cups of *tteokbokki* and thin discs of dalgona (sponge toffee) to hungry schoolkids in front of elementary schools. In nightlife districts, patrons sit at plastic tables in large tent restaurants called *pojangmacha* while proprieters cook up comfort food such as *kalguksu* (knife-cut noodle soup) and *pajeon* (green onion pancakes).

Street food is a social unifier. Regardless of a person's social status or what part of the country they're from, everyone grew up eating staples like *tteokbokki* and *odeng* (fishcake), and remembers them with equal fondness. And that's the beauty of Korea's dining-out culture: bringing the country together through a shared love of great food.

Late-night bites

Koreans frequently work, study or drink late into the night, and to satisfy after-hours cravings they turn to *yasik*, or late-night food. While the simplest and cheapest choice is a quick bowl of *ramyeon* (instant noodles) from a convenience store, the most popular delivery option is *chimaek*, a combination of *chikin* (fried chicken) and *maekju* (beer). Other common *yasik* include *tteokbokki*, *jokbal* (pork trotters) and *dakbal* (chicken feet), the latter prepared very spicy – all the better for stress relief, given the release of endorphins.

명절 음식
Holiday food

For many, the best signature dishes are those that mark signature moments – a life milestone, a national holiday or an anniversary.

If food is about families coming together, the *jesa* table takes it one step further. A ceremonial food spread, a *jesa* is an ancient memorial honouring ancestors, and is held at different times of the year, from certain holidays to the anniversary of the death of a loved one. Since the spread features foods that one's ancestors enjoyed, the dishes on a *jesa* table vary by family and region. As many as 30 dishes tend to cram a *jesa* table, creating a vibrant display of meats, side dishes, fruit and alcohol.

It's not always about putting on a huge spread, though; sometimes one special dish can do all the talking. During Lunar New Year, many people eat the savoury soup *tteokguk*, made with flat, white rice cakes that represent purity and a fresh start to a new year. At Chuseok *(p107)*, families make or buy the steamed rice cake *songpyeon*; superstition says that a woman who makes pretty *songpyeon* will meet a good husband. And on individual birthdays, it's the custom to eat the seaweed soup *miyeokguk*, which pays tribute to a time when mothers consumed it just after giving birth for its nutritional benefits.

Beyond an excuse to feast, holiday and ceremonial foods are tied up in strong symbolism, and provide a window into customs and beliefs that Koreans hold dear.

Making *songpyeon* for Chuseok, Busan

Signature drinks

Tangy teas, sweet rice wines, fruity spirits: whether they act as a pick-me-up, a social bonder or a soul soother, Korea's homegrown tipples are in a class of their own.

Korea's drinks, much like its food, are defined by their flavours: spicy or sour, sweet or pungent, roasted or bitter. Whatever the flavour, there's a drink for every occasion and every moment.

A daily routine

For many, the passage of time is marked by the beverages that are consumed. In the mornings, the aroma of freshly ground beans takes over hip cafés, where friends catch up over iced Americanos or lattes.

For lunch, restaurants serve chilled barley tea with food, and after school, students scour convenience store shelves for Milkis soda – a born-in-Korea soft drink. Come evening, alcohol becomes the tipple of choice. At *hofs* (beer halls), college students order icy glasses of Korean Cass or Hite beers with their fried chicken. Raucous groups of colleagues fill barbecue restaurants, starting on their first round of drinks before the grilled meat is cooked and paired with soju or *makgeolli*. The next morning, digestive cures like Bacchus or Hwal Myung Su are sipped on the way to work, starting a new day.

Outside of the everyday, if there's an occasion to be had, there's a drink almost made for it. For those relaxing at a *jjimjilbang* (p115), *sikhye* – a cold sweetened dessert rice drink – is a refresher. In fancier settings, business negotiations are made over expensive liquors like plum wine. All in all, drinks are yet another excuse to indulge in Korea's incredible flavours.

Preparing multiple brews at a sleek coffee shop in Seoul

1 Soju paired with Korean dishes

2 Tea master preparing a pot of tea in Jeonju

3 The retro rice wine, *makgeolli*

4 Cass, a popular *maekju* brand

5 *Dongdongju* scooped from a bowl with a large wooden ladle

6 Brewing coffee at a stylish café

Korea arguably excels when it comes to producing alcohol, but that's not to say non-alcoholic drinks are given any less love. From traditional teas to experimental spirits, there's a drink for every meal or mood.

Soju

Translated as "burnt liquor", soju is the alcohol of choice for Koreans, and goes with any meal. First popularized during the 14th century, the clear drink is made from fermenting grains or other starches, and its alcohol content ranges from 12 to 45 per cent. While mass-produced – Chamisul, found in green bottles on supermarket shelves and in restaurants, is a favourite – soju is also made by artisans, using a range of traditional distillation methods.

Tea

There's very little that tea – a staple since the Silla era – doesn't go with. Refreshing cold barley tea, which has a grainy flavour, is typically served with lunch, while *maesil-cha*, a dessert tea made from green plum extract, doubles up as the perfect tangy summer drink. In the winter, *yuja-cha*, made from citrus fruit, is mixed with *yuja* preserves, sugar and water for a soothing drink.

Makgeolli

Also known as *takju*, this milky-white fermented rice wine has been brewed in Korea for over 2,000 years. Ranging from 6 to 18 per cent alcohol content, it has a sweet flavour, and consists of the cloudier alcohol that sinks to the bottom during the fermentation process. While it was a drink for the working classes in the Joseon era, *makgeolli* has seen a resurgence in the 21st century; today, it's often sipped between bites of *pajeon* (green onion pancakes) on rainy days.

Maekju

Beer *(maekju)* was first introduced in the early 20th century, with breweries opening in 1908. Popular Korean brands include Cass, Hite and Terra, but for many, *somaek* is the highlight of the beer scene – a mix of three parts soju to seven parts *maekju*. A favourite way to enjoy an icy pint is to pair it with crispy fried chicken – a combo that's been named *chimaek* (chicken and *maekju*).

Dongdongju

While it can be categorized as *makgeolli* in its younger, premature state, *dongdongju* is thicker, less fermented and less filtered. Rice kernels float to the top, making for a grittier drink that's sweet yet subtly tart in flavour. It's a Korean pastime to enjoy a cool bowlful after a hike.

Coffee

Experimenting with unexpected flavours is at the forefront of the coffee scene. The standard morning fare is the A-a (the phonetic nickname for iced Americano), but coffee shops also sell variations of the likes of nutty multigrain or roasted sweet potato lattes. Cappuccinos, meanwhile, are often lattes coated with cinnamon. Korea is also one of the largest consumers of instant coffee in the world.

음주 문화

Drink culture

Much like food, the culture of drinking is a means through which Korean values are expressed: honouring ancestors, celebrating the land and forming societal bonds.

When settling in for a meal, tables are often crammed with bottles of soju or beer that are clinked and swashed between bites of food. While tea and coffee have a strong place in the drinks scene, it's *sul* (alcohol) that is the mainstay of Korea's drinking culture, marking social occasions and honouring special events.

Brewing it up

Beverages have reflected Korea's geography and climate since the founding of the Goguryeo kingdom. For farmers around the country,

Drinks with a view at a rooftop bar in Busan

drinks marked seasonal changes; once harvests ended, leftover grains would be used to brew alcohol for the winter. Over the centuries, each region developed a special process of fermentation that added a unique flair to its alcohol, but for the lower classes and farmers, *makgeolli* was the drink of choice. Known as *nonju*, or "farmer's liquor", it would be drunk in the morning with breakfast before farmers headed to the fields.

Alcohol was, however, much more than something to drink. For the Chuseok harvest festival, families would pay respects to ancestral graves by bearing gifts of fruits and alcohol. On the death anniversaries of ancestors, *cheongju* – a clear rice wine – was considered a medium for communicating with the spirits and asking for good fortune. Like food, alcohol was also used to ward off illnesses. Special types of soju, such as *dosoju*, brewed with medicinal herbs, were consumed to drive out diseases and evil spirits during Lunar New Year.

In the spirit

During the Joseon dynasty, many households fermented and produced their own alcohol. By the early 20th century, industrialized breweries came to the fore. The distinction between liquors drunk by different classes disappeared, and previously "upper-class" alcohols, such as soju, became cheaper and commonly sold. Drinking became an accepted part of every

Drink with decorum

There's a hierarchy to drinking, especially when there's a mix of different ages at the table. When accepting a drink from an elder, hold the glass with both hands; when pouring a drink for an elder, hold the bottle with one hand and your forearm with the other to show respect. The youngest person is responsible for making sure that glasses are never empty.

occasion, with little stigma attached to getting inebriated. When Imperial Japan occupied Korea in 1910, however, they imposed a hefty alcohol tax; home-made liquor was soon outlawed, meaning only those with licences could produce it. Korea continued to suppress its alcohol production levels after the Korean War, when grain shortages were an issue. After decades of economic recovery, the government lifted all restrictions in the 1990s, and brewing culture re-emerged in full force.

Today, alcohol types range from daily drinks with meals to pricier, specially fermented brews. Most common are soju, *makgeolli*, *yakju*, *cheongju* and *dongdongju*. On special occasions, elders may prefer more traditional spirits such as *bokbunjaju*, *meoruju* and *maesilju*, brewed from fruits or grains. Following Korea's exposure to Western culture, wine and spirits such as whiskey and Scotch have also become popular.

Where there's alcohol, there are drinking snacks. *Anju*, which can be roughly translated to "food to be consumed with alcohol", serves as a side to the main event. Common *anju* are dried squid, peanuts or seafood pancakes. At *pojangmacha* (covered food stalls), spicy rice cakes or chicken gizzards are paired with soju or *makgeolli*.

A pressured society

The hefty focus on alcohol doesn't come without its problems. Korea has the highest rates of alcohol drinking in Asia, with around 10.9 litres consumed per head per year, followed by Vietnam at 8.7 litres. One of the reasons for these figures could be the general pressure to drink, with alcohol commonly deemed a social and professional necessity, and a way to strengthen

건배
Geonbae
The Korean word for "cheers", meaning "empty glass", has Chinese character roots.

interpersonal relationships. Such is alcohol's dominance that there's a concept of "learning alcohol" from family elders when one comes of drinking age: learning how to swallow the bitter taste, or the rules surrounding drinking etiquette. Drinking is also cemented as a staple of the dining scene, and has become a huge part of after-work company gatherings, known as *hoesik*.

Increasingly, however, there's been a vocal backlash against this culture of pressured consumption. The dangers of pushing people to drink has been raised by Korea's health ministry, which has been actively promoting lower, healthier levels of alcohol intake among adults. Many young people, meanwhile, are keen to explore social experiences that do not revolve around drinking.

Dalgona coffee

This famed whipped coffee took off as a social media trend during the COVID-19 pandemic, when DIY TikToks and YouTube videos making the drink went viral. Dalgona coffee, which takes its name from the Korean sugar candy, is made by whipping together instant coffee powder, sugar and water until frothy and creamy. A milk of choice is added at the end, and the drink can be topped with honey or cocoa.

Coffee shop culture

While low- or zero-alcohol alternatives are few and far between, for those who don't want to drink alcohol, Korea's coffee culture is a welcome reprieve. Seoul famously has more coffee shops per capita than Seattle – the hometown of Starbucks® – at around 17 cafés per 10,000 citizens.

Though Starbucks® has become the top player in Korea's coffee market (Korea has the fourth largest amount of Starbucks® in the world), most cafés are either independently owned or part of a Korean chain, such as A Twosome Place. Some cafés are even themed.

Coffee didn't arrive in Korea until 1896, when it was first tasted by King Gojong. The drink represented a move towards modernization, and the first Korean cafés shot up at the start of the 20th century. For a long time, this new import could only be afforded by the upper classes. But as more cafés opened up post-Korean War, coffee fast became a favourite for everyone, from salespeople to students. Today, Seoul is home to entire streets dedicated to cafés, where people spend the day hopping between coffee shos or whiling away the hours in their favourite spot.

Younger people are increasingly finding that settling in with a hot brew is just as conducive to social bonding as drinking at a bar. And coffee isn't limited to early starts: as a standard post-meal beverage, most restaurants offer instant vending machine coffees on the house, a sugary-sweet drink that acts as a staple dessert and palate cleanser.

Socializing over drinks in the evening

KOREA IS
KICKING BACK

Koreans have a reputation for working extremely long hours, be it studying until midnight to get into a top university or going above and beyond to rise through the ranks of a top company. But as much as Koreans work hard, they play hard, too. Until 2004, the working week was six days long, with only one precious day off to rest, relax and recoup. Now that it's been extended to two days for the majority of the population, you'll find Koreans making the most of their time off, playing e-sports at PC *bang*, grooving to their favourite songs at *noraebang* and enjoying some retail therapy. And while many choose to hike high peaks or cycle vast stretches of the country, others find pleasure in sitting back to watch major sports events from the comfort of their home. Koreans certainly know how to make the most of downtime.

옷가게

코스메틱

커피 와플 카페

종합 광고 기획

안경 렌즈

빙수 떡 카

Celebrating the
Buddha's birth at the
Lotus Lantern Festival

한국의 축제들

Korean festivals

Korea's rich history and vibrant culture come to life in a host of festivals celebrated throughout the year. These cultural markers offer Koreans a welcome excuse to come together and celebrate.

Korea may be noted for its non-stop work ethos, but when holidays come along, the partying takes over. In fact, work is officially suspended across Korea when beloved public holidays come around.

Evolution of celebrations

In an increasingly modern society, festivals are key to preserving fading traditions. Many of Korea's festivals honour the country's agricultural roots. Before industrialization sparked an economic boom after the Korean War, Korea suffered extreme poverty. Farming was the primary source of living and events were focused on praying for and celebrating a fruitful harvest.

Though many people don't identify with a religion (p44), Korea also celebrates a number of religious festivals – such as the Buddha's

Birthday and the shamanistic Andong Mask Dance Festival. These are inclusive events and the non-religious often partake, too.

As global influences reached Korea, newer festivals entered the calendar (albeit with Korean culture at their very heart). Parents are given carnations on Parents' Day – a combination of Mother's Day and Father's Day. Christmas, meanwhile, involves friends and couples eating out rather than families feasting at home. Several other cultural festivals, such as the Busan International Film Festival, also sprung up after democratization in the 1990s.

Ultimately, Korea's festivals are a vibrant mix of traditional and contemporary ceremonies. Whether they originated abroad or were born out of home-grown customs, they celebrate the values that Koreans hold dear.

1 Lanterns floating along the river in Jinju

2 Making *songpyeon* during Chuseok

3 Temple decorated for Buddha's Birthday

4 Participants at Boryeong Mud Festival

5 A lively parade for Lunar New Year

From abundant autumnal harvest feasts to glorious lantern displays, Korea's most popular festivals bring the country together in celebration of its storied history.

Jinju Lantern Festival

The roots of this spectacular festival stretch back through the centuries. It pays homage to the lanterns that were used as part of a military strategy in the Jinjuseong Fortress Battle of the Imjin War (1592–1598). During this time, lanterns were floated across the Nam River to keep Japanese troops from crossing; today, every October, lanterns are again set adrift along the river in the city of Jinju. Fireworks displays, water shows and cultural performances also take place.

Chuseok (Korean Thanksgiving)

Also known as Hangawi, Chuseok is one of the biggest holidays in the country. Held on the 15th day of the eighth month of the lunar calendar, the three-day event sees families gather to appreciate one another and their ancestors via *jesa* ceremonies *(p92)*, known as *charye* during Chuseok and Seollal (Lunar New Year). The bountiful harvest is also celebrated. Many families buy or make *songpyeon*, a special rice cake, to enjoy for the occasion.

Buddha's Birthday

Also known as the "Day When Buddha Came", this festival is observed on the eighth day of the fourth month of the lunar calendar. Various events take place across the country, including masked dance performances, parades and traditional games. Colourful candlelit paper lanterns are used to decorate various temples – those celebrating can write their name and a desired wish on a paper tag to hang from the bottom of the lantern.

Boryeong Mud Festival

This annual summer festival, which draws the country's largest number of international visitors, was born from a small marketing promotion in 1994. The event aimed to resurrect the struggling economy of Boryeong by promoting the rich mineral mud – from the city's Daecheon Beach – as a cosmetic product. Its unexpected success launched this riotous festival, which involves everything from mud massages to messy, mud-throwing activities.

Seollal (Lunar New Year)

Ringing in the new year according to the lunar calendar (a calendar based on the moon's phases), Seollal sees extended families gather to share delicious food, such as a bowl of *tteokguk* (which symbolizes new beginnings), play traditional games and pass on ancestral rites *(charye)* over a *jesa* table. People don hanbok, the traditional Korean garment, and younger family members perform a bowing ritual (known as *saebae*) to demonstrate respect for their elders. The elders then share words of wisdom for the year and hand out money for good luck and fortune.

(리테일 테라피)

Retail therapy

For a trend-focused country, it's not surprising that shopping is a national pastime, whether browsing stores to test out the latest products or spending the weekend splashing out online.

Korea has come a long way since the days of the humble market pedlar. Progress in the retail sector continues at speed, with a proliferation of glitzy malls vying with online stores.

Love of the new

Shop-till-you-drop culture is relatively new in Korea. It was only

in the late 18th century that people set up shop at *oiljang* (markets held every five days). As living standards improved and disposable income increased throughout the 1970s and 80s, fashion came to the forefront. The desire to own the latest clothes and gadgets became embedded in the fabric of an increasingly capitalistic society, and hyper-consumerism was born, with large malls springing up rapidly to service increased consumer demand.

Today, the number of credit cards per Korean household is up there with the highest in the world, testament to a love of spending. Urban malls have been joined by rural outlets, too, as space for large complexes is limited in Korea's dense cities.

Above Shopping at the Hyundai Seoul department store

Left A Korean merchant carrying goods on his back, late 19th century

& GO

[NICE WEATHER]

LIFESTYLE GOODS

ZERO/ZERO

UNCOMMON ITEMS

GN GOODS

Instant gratification

Innovative online stores now threaten physical malls, however, by capitalizing on the demand for speed. Consumers seek the endorphin rush of seeing the latest face product in their home within a matter of hours, without having to leave the house. Some pioneering stores even ensure that deliveries are received before 7am the next day.

Surprisingly for a society that reveres the new, attitudes towards second-hand goods are changing, thanks in part to online sites like Danggeun Market. A popular platform for buying and selling used goods, the site is a game-changer for retail, encouraging consumers to cease chasing the next big thing.

Korean products

Cosmetics
Blockbuster chains like Amorepacific provide miracle creams and moisturizing face masks.

Electronics
Gadgets are mostly bought online, though Seoul's two Techno Mart malls continue to do brisk business.

Fabrics
Many markets have shops making colourful bespoke hanbok (traditional Korean outfits).

Bamboo goods
Along with woven bamboo baskets, some stores sell huggable bamboo pillows called "bamboo wives".

Pottery
Replicas of celadon masterpieces are sold at Icheon Ceramics Village and tourist shops.

Masks
Expressive wooden masks are used in traditional dances, some still performed in Andong.

다양한 야외 활동

The great outdoors

Despite the country's swift urbanization, Koreans retain an intimate connection to nature. Escaping to the outdoors not only provides exercise, but is also a restorative balm for the soul.

Even before the six-day working week was shortened to five in 2004, Koreans made time to connect with the world beyond their walls. With thousands of hiking trails and 22 national parks, Korea offers plenty of options for enjoying the natural world.

On land

Given that 70 per cent of Korea is mountainous, it's perhaps unsurprising that hiking is a favourite pastime. City dwellers can reach many trails by metro, and the peaks are often packed every

weekend. Trails range from the leisurely, like the Jeju Olle Trail that follows Jeju Island's coastline, to the strenuous, such as the climb up Dobongsan's Jaunbong Peak, which involves an elevation gain of 645 m (2,116 ft).

Hiking might be Korea's most widespread pursuit, but opportunities for cycling also abound, with cutting-edge racing bikes speeding along the nation's riverside paths. The Cross-Country Cycling Road network, seen by many as the gold standard in Korean cycling routes, comprises long-distance paths; the country's serious cyclists tackle the route between Seoul and Busan. Casual riders can be seen on rented city bikes, and leisurely rail bikes (those pedalled along tracks) are popular in places like Uiwang.

On the water

Though Korea is a peninsula with thousands of islands, relatively few citizens are confident swimmers. This may be due to a dearth of learning facilities, with only one

Right A surfer takes to the waves off the coast of Jeju island

Below The rocky peak of Dobongsan, just north of Seoul

per cent of schools having access to a swimming pool. Koreans are still very much drawn to the sea, however, and make good use of the short beach season, which tends to last from early July to late August, after which most facilities close as the weather turns.

Surfing has become a booming subculture, and has transformed some of the country's quiet fishing villages into pulsing centres of youthful activity. While some surfers seek out competitions, other cherish the chance to unwind with friends on the surging water. Though waves are in short supply during the warmer months, with the coming of typhoons in early autumn, the surf picks up, and surfers visit popular surfing beaches near Busan or Yangyang on the east coast.

Further inland, Korea's rivers are often used by waterskiers and rafters. As the icy Siberian winds freeze the waterways, counties like Hwacheon hold ice fishing festivals and children try *seolmae* (traditional ice sledding) at places like the Yongin Folk Village. Whatever the weather, the natural world is ingrained in Korean recreation, and the varied landscape is the perfect backdrop to the nation's downtime.

Camping and glamping

Koreans enjoy the pleasures of camping, but rarely in the wilderness. They venture instead to campgrounds, which become fully booked months in advance. For comfort-loving glampers, power outlets, showers and cooking areas come as standard, with an array of luxuries enjoyed, from fires to movie projectors.

1 Bicycles and blossoms, Jinhae Gunhangje Festival

2 Parents swimming with children on Jeju Island

3 Diving off the coast of Jeju Island

4 Skiers and snowboarders in Deogyusan

SEASONAL ACTIVITIES

With its muggy summers and frigid winters, its vast mountain ranges and strings of sandy beaches, Korea is well suited for warm-water activities, intrepid snow sports and everything in between.

Spring

The spring signals a re-emergence from the cold winter, with windows thrown open and a new season of activities beginning. Many welcome the start of flower-gazing season from April, when the appearance of lush blossom sees crowds gather to enjoy forsythia, azalea, magnolia and cherry blossoms. Looking for blossoms can involve hiking up a steep peak or simply visiting a city park. Mornings can still be brisk in March and April, however, and *kkotsaemchuwi* (cold spells in late spring) necessitate warmer clothing for walks or treks.

Summer

Summers are hot, humid and unpredictable, with a substantial amount of rainfall. Koreans defy the energy-draining temperatures (which rage hottest in July and August) by visiting coastal spots and islands, with subtropical Jeju Island popular. On the west coast, families dig for sea creatures in the expansive mudflats; to the east, several large caverns offer cool intermissions from beach lounging. An inland pastime during the dog days is visiting mountain valleys *(gyegok),* naturally air conditioned by limpid streams. Some *gyegok* have open-air restaurants dotted along the streambanks.

Autumn

By late October, the maples are turning crimson, and wide temperature differences between morning and afternoon determine which activities are undertaken, and when. The crisp mornings are perfect for road marathons and trail-running races, such as the 9 Peaks race through the swaying silvergrass of the Yeongnam Alps. Early autumn is also a good time for scuba diving, and many visit the dive centres scattered along the east coast to enjoy the tepid waters. Though it's becoming rarer, some still learn to dive the traditional way without an air tank, by taking an introductory course at one of Jeju Island's two *haenyeo* (female free-diver) schools *(p24).*

Winter

As strong winds blow in from Siberia, winter becomes extremely cold, and the northern regions are blanketed in snow. For some, the cold season can seem interminable, and hibernating is the only option. For winter-sport enthusiasts, however, a new season of outdoor fun begins. By far the most popular winter sports are skiing and snowboarding, with about 20 resorts dotted around the country. What really sets Korean ski resorts apart is their night skiing. Visitors can arrive straight after work for some vital relief on the slopes, and nights often feature sundown events including DJs and fireworks. Many resorts offer cheaper passes for select runs that stay open and well-illuminated until as late as 4am.

찜질방

Jjimjilbang

Though *jjimjilbang* literally means "room where heat is applied", these fixtures of Korean culture are more than spa pools and sauna chambers. Multistorey emporiums of relaxation, their amenities can include massage chairs, gyms, snack counters, *manhwa* (manga) comic rooms and sleeping areas. Night and day blend together in a *jjimjilbang*, and some visitors while away hours in their cosy confines.

Before modern *jjimjilbang*, every neighbourhood had a *mogyoktang*, a simple bathhouse serving a social as well as a hygienic function. The need for *mogyoktang* dwindled as more people began living in apartments with bathing fixtures, though these bathhouses can still be found in some cities and towns. *Jjimjilbang* are grander versions of *mogyoktang*, and though some people are regulars, most visitors are content to visit as a relaxing treat once a month or so.

Upon entering a *jjimjilbang*, an admission fee is paid in exchange for a locker key and a loose-fitting outfit. Men and women then enter separate locker rooms, undress and take a shower. Scratchy exfoliating towels are on hand for scrubbing off *ttae* (grime and dead skin particles). It's then time to dip into the hot and cold baths – some infused with therapeutic agents like green tea – or enter a sauna room. Finally, some visitors wind down on mats in the communal sleeping rooms. After just a couple of hours in a *jjimjilbang*, one emerges into the outside world feeling as good as new.

Relaxing on sleeping mats within a *jjimjilbang*

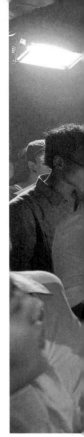

해 지 고 난 후

After dark

Whether it's a midweek singing session or a trip to an online gaming den, nights out take leisure time to the extreme, and offer a much-needed reprieve from long working days.

Widely known for their rigorous work routines and intense study schedules, Koreans often crave a release come nightfall. It's no surprise, then, that entertainment in the small hours comes in many forms and caters to a range of interests. Fun is not limited to the weekends, with something on every night of the week. As the nation winds down, venues open their doors and Koreans kick back in style.

Nights out

For many, a quintessential night out progresses through a unique series of *cha*, or rounds. As the soju flows, the night comes alive with shared joy, and the day's struggles are put firmly out of mind. For 1-*cha*, round one, friends might meet at a grilled meat restaurant, where beef or pork is cooked at the table between bottles of soju. Next, 2-*cha* could involve a trip to a lively craft beer bar, or a trendy *makgeolli* pub. Here, drinks will often be bought in rounds, with everyone contributing their share. Those looking to take the night to 3-*cha* might catch a taxi to a university district thronged with nightclubs or live music venues, or a retro-style LP bar, where drinkers can make song requests while nursing beer or whiskey.

Many nights will culminate at the cornerstone of Korean nightlife: the *noraebang* (singing room). In private rooms replete with huge screens

and disco balls, partygoers of all ages belt out hits with friends, decompressing with the help of a microphone and a varied queue of tunes. Leaving the *noraebang*, the night might wind down at a *pojangmacha* (covered food stall) for nibbles and a nightcap.

Business outings

While some nights out offer an escape from the rigours of the working week, others can seem an extension of it. Dreaded by many, revered by others, team or company dinners *(hoesik)* are a part of working life, and it's considered rude to skip them. *Hoesik* may be held every week or only once or twice a year to

Convenience stores

The cheapest alfresco bars in Korea happen to be convenience stores, which are especially popular in small towns. An array of drinkers – including labourers, nightshift workers, and tourists – congregate on these stores' patios, which have plastic chairs and tables protected by awnings. The stores offer a wide selection of foreign beers and local tipples like soju and *makgeolli,* as well as a range of cheap snacks. The sidewalk vantages make for great people-watching.

Above Live music at a club in Hongdae district, Seoul

Left A private room at a *noraebang*

Drinking games

Younger Koreans will often kickstart their nights with a spot of amiable competition.

Bottle cap game
The twisty appendage of a soju cap is flicked; the person who breaks it must drink.

Intuition game
Players shout out a number; losers are those who say the same number or are too slow.

Sam-yuk-gu
Participants count up, clapping for numbers containing 3, 6 or 9. Mistakes result in shots.

Baskin Robbins 31
The drinkers take turns counting up, saying up to three numbers. The one who reaches 31, drinks.

Submarine game
Players pour soju into a shot glass within a glass of beer. Sinking it means drinking it.

welcome a new employee. They start out rather formal, with speeches from bosses, and can bring into play Confucian-inspired rules of seniority (pouring a drink with two hands to show respect, for example).

Once the speeches conclude, however, *hoesik* offer a great opportunity to cultivate friendships with favoured colleagues, or to review the working day. While some may feel pressured to drink too much soju, some others dilute their beer or soju with water, perhaps even pouring their drinks away, in order not to lose face with colleagues – or feel thick-headed in the morning.

Similar in many ways are *jeopdae* (dinner and drinks with clients). These generally take place at swankier establishments, with corporate deals and the business of the day discussed over a few bottles of premium imported whiskey.

Above Enjoying Korean barbecue after work, Seoul

Right Eating noodles at a PC *bang*

Escape into fantasy

The after-dark scene isn't limited to going out and drinking. In towns and cities, there are often thousands of popular internet cafés, known as PC *bang*, which offer a range of online games. These facilities attract gamers of all ages, mainly with the escapist lure of massive multiplayer online role-playing games (MMORPGs).

Long gone are the days when PC *bang* were housed in dark basements dense with cigarette smoke, offering little besides spicy ramen and sugary vending machine coffee. Today, denizens enjoy state-of-the-art facilities including ultra-high-speed internet, top-of-the-range head- phones and ergonomic chairs. Gamers can stay all night if they wish, as PC *bang* are open 24 hours. It's even possible to order a full meal at a cheap price, without so much as glancing away from the fantasy unfolding on screen. Though many gamers are now content to stay at home with their own consoles (as household internet speeds get ever faster), PC *bang* still provide a semblance of social life for those who need it, or simply offer a quieter alternative to the rowdy nightlife unfolding beyond.

Winding down

The Korean reverence for productivity and motivation certainly meets its match in the value placed upon collective joy come nightfall. Whether it's a night-long marathon of revelry or a simple game with friends, nights out mean cooling off and chilling out. If there's one thing that Koreans love to get right, it's a good night out.

Sporting success

Life in Korea is competitive, and this drive has helped produce an incredible sporting scene, one that has brought the country global recognition and served as an immense source of pride.

Koreans' affinity for sports seems natural, considering that so many traits possessed by elite athletes apply just as well to the Korean character: proud, competitive and driven to succeed. Evidence of this drive is everywhere – public schools host annual sports days, driving ranges perch atop office roofs and coin-operated punching bags dot the streets of nightlife districts – and watching sports is more than just casual fandom.

Rising up

For such a small country, Korea has made a massive mark in the world of sports. In fact, the consistent achievements of short-track speed skaters, archers and golfers are every bit as celebrated as K-pop's global success.

Korea's accomplishments are all the more remarkable for the nation's underdog status. Sporting success is reliant upon economic success; developing top-tier leagues and infrastructure are costly endeavours. In this regard Korea was behind early on, having spent half of the 20th century under a repressive colonial regime and then being decimated in a civil war. As the country battled back and developed its economy, it found the requisite stability and funds to invest in world-class athletic facilities and player development. Today, every Korean gold medal and international championship is a proud reminder of how far the country has come.

But sports are about more than just national pride. They're also an avenue for the country to apply its technological prowess, as it did in pioneering professional e-sports leagues (p199). Whether watching or playing them, sports are a release from the pressures of cram schools and long working hours. And, in a culture where friendships are often formed through formal organizations like university clubs and work teams, they provide a way to create and

Lee Dae-hoon (left) during the men's-68 kg taekwondo final, 2014 Asian Games

Major sporting events

From defying the odds during times of strife to achieving global fame, Korea has firmly established itself on the sporting stage.

1920

The Joseon Sports Council is founded to host and sponsor athletic competitions, increasing public interest in sports.

1936

Sohn Kee-chung becomes the first Korean to win Olympic gold (though he's forced to compete for Japan) – in the marathon.

1988

Seoul hosts the Summer Olympics, an event that has transformative effects on Korea's sports and politics.

1966

The Korea National Training Center is established to develop the country's athletes.

2002

Korea co-hosts the football World Cup with Japan and makes it to the semifinals, the furthest an Asian team has ever progressed.

2005

Park Young-seok is the first to climb both the Seven Summits and all 14 8,000-m (26,000-ft) peaks, and trek to both poles.

2022

Footballer Son Heung-min wins the English Premier League Golden Boot, ending the season with 23 goals.

2018

Pyeongchang hosts the Winter Olympics; Korea finishes with 17 medals, its highest Winter Games tally.

2010

Kim Yuna wins gold in women's figure skating at the Vancouver Winter Olympics, setting a world points record.

strengthen social bonds. More than 10 per cent of Koreans are members of an athletic club.

The soul of sports

While imports like baseball and soccer dominate the contemporary scene, Korea's competitive traditions lie in its martial arts. Today, this heritage is carried on primarily through taekwondo. Surprisingly, taekwondo is a rather modern – even bureaucratic – creation that's less than 100 years old. After World War II, martial arts schools called gwan began to appear, each teaching its own unique fighting style. In the mid-1950s, several gwan began to merge their styles with the goal of creating a unified Korean martial art. The process resulted in what would become known as taekwondo.

While the sport has gone global, becoming an Olympic event in 2000, it remains firmly enmeshed in Korean society. Every youngster gets a taste of it in school physical education classes, and many kids practise it at private academies, of which there were more than 10,000 in 2020. Korean soldiers also train in the discipline.

Modern taekwondo is the spiritual heir of taekkyeon, which is considered Korea's oldest martial art, dating to the Three Kingdoms era. Fluid and rhythmic, taekkyeon almost looks like a dance, involving constant motion of both hands and feet. The martial art largely served as a leisure pursuit for the working class, with villagers bonding at competitions held during holidays. Prohibited during the Japanese colonial period, taekkyeon was revived, almost single-handedly, by the taekkyeon master Song Duk-ki. Today, relatively few Koreans practise taekkyeon, but it's no longer in danger of disappearing; in 2011, it became the first martial art to receive UNESCO Intangible Cultural Heritage status.

Another UNESCO-listed martial art with ancient origins, ssireum (p125) has transitioned from military training activity to popular pastime. The first professional tournaments were held in the 1910s, and by the 1970s, a number of pro teams were forming. In 1997, however, the Asian financial crisis stifled the sport's development, and ssireum reverted to an amateur pursuit. Still, it remains a much-loved part of Korean sporting culture, with televised tournaments held on major holidays and impromptu ssireum matches breaking out during family gatherings. Koreans might gravitate towards modern sports today, but martial arts will long have their place in this culture.

Inspiring art

Throughout the centuries, ssireum was frequently the subject of folk paintings. The most famous of these is a 1784 work, titled "Ssireum", by Joseon painter Kim Hong-do. The painting depicts a scene that feels contemporary: a crowd watching two men grapple, while a vendor walks around selling candy.

1 Archer Kang Chae-young competing at the 2020 Olympics

2 *Ssireum* wrestlers competing in Andong

3 A taekwondo bout at the 2020 Olympics

4 Football starSon Heung-min

5 Fans supporting the Doosan Bears baseball team, Seoul

SIGNATURE SPORTS

Korea's diverse sporting scene comprises the traditional and the new, the global and the home-grown. Athletes have found success in a huge array of disciplines, though some sports are national favourites.

Archery

This centuries-old tradition is so iconic that both the sport and the craft of making bows and arrows are designated National Intangible Cultural Properties. Today, Korean archers dominate international competition. This is especially true of the female athletes, who have won nine of the past ten individual Olympic gold medals, 19 of 30 individual Olympic medals awarded since 1984, and every Olympic team gold there's ever been (1988–2021).

Ssireum

In the ancient wrestling form of *ssireum*, wrestlers latch onto their opponent's *satba* – a sash worn around the waist and one thigh – and attempt to force any part of their body above the knee to the ground. Unlike in Japanese sumo, blows are not allowed, and forcing an opponent out of the sand ring merits only a restart. Winners were traditionally awarded an ox. Today, many women have taken up what used to be a male-only sport.

Taekwondo

No sport is as closely associated with Korea as taekwondo. Korean martial artists developed the sport in the 1940s and 50s, drawing on karate, wushu and ancient Korean martial arts like *taekkyeon* to create a sport that emphasizes athletic kicks, speed and respect for others. In Olympic taekwondo, athletes commence matches with a bow and score points by landing punches or kicks to their opponent's head and torso.

Football

Korea's love affair with football dates to 1882, when British sailors are thought to have introduced the sport at the port of Incheon. Today, the K League is arguably Asia's best domestic competition, its teams having won the AFC Champions League a record 12 times. On the global stage, the men's national team has appeared at every World Cup since 1986, a streak that includes a fairy-tale run to the semifinals in 2002. Korea has also birthed some of the world's premier individual talents, notably Son Heung-min and Ji So-yun, both household names among global football fans.

Baseball

The Korea Baseball Organization is the country's most popular sports league, and stadiums are packed all summer. The KBO is far less buttoned-up than its US counterpart, Major League Baseball, with cheer squads leading raucous fans in coordinated chants, and the post-home run bat flip – taboo in MLB – being a delightfully disrespectful art form here. Korean ballplayers have found plenty of international success, too, with many making it to the big leagues, and the national team winning gold at the 2008 Olympics.

KOREA IS

TELLING STORIES

Korea's story is not confined to the history books – it permeates every aspect of art and culture, be that theatre, literature, design or fashion. Between conflicting early kingdoms, Japanese colonial occupation and the Korean War, this is a country that has gone through devastation and upheaval and – despite looking fearlessly to a brighter future – refuses to forget its origins. And while the likes of books and plays are literally telling the story of Korea, you'll also find it where you least expect it – for example in the joyful murals that have boosted the appearance of ramshackle villages in recent years, the innovative architecture that's come to define city skylines and the experimental fashion that dominates both streets and catwalks. Ever reflective, ever evolving, the stories of Korea are still being written.

예술적 정체성

Artistic identities

From sublime ceramics to cutting-edge media installations, Koreans have cultivated a dynamic artistic character, inheriting and reworking an array of global influences in the process.

Art has always run far deeper than decoration. Traditionally, delicate handicrafts attested to the allure of ritual and religion, before other national styles began to infuse Korea's creative palette. Today, these influences have been beautifully adapted, and centuries of creativity yield insights into Korea's history, culture and place in the world.

Early forms

Traditional Korean art spanned an array of crafts, including metalwork, jade carving, sculpture and pottery.

The greatest early treasures speak volumes about the centrality of religion, from mystical Seokguram Grotto carvings to Bodhisattva sculptures.

Ink painting on paper or silk came to Korea by way of China in the Goryeo era (918–1392). The Chinese-inspired landscapes painted in black ink typically depicted grandiose rocky peaks, with humans barely figuring in the scenes. Masterful control of different brushes was needed to create atmospheric strokes denoting mist-shrouded cliffs, as well as the intricate details of trees. While technical prowess was important, creating a contemplative effect in the mind of the viewer was what counted. Only in the 18th century did Korean painters trailblaze new styles by depicting sublime local panoramas like Mount Kumgang rather than famous Chinese landscapes in derivative forms.

The Joseon period (1392–1910) saw the adoption of a new style of still life painting called the *sagunja*, or the "four gentlemen". These paintings featured four plants – bamboo, plum blossom, orchid and chrysanthemum – to symbolize neo-Confucian virtues such as humility, perseverance and purity. Other important paintings of the Joseon era were *minhwa* (folk paintings), produced by working-class artists to bring good fortune to ordinary homes. Most *minhwa* were painted on *hanji* (traditional Korean paper made from mulberry bark) and recalled old folktales often featuring powerful animals such as tigers. *Minhwa* began fading during the Korean War

Below Painting depicting a tiger, Bongeunsa Temple in Seoul

Right Fine embroidery patch on a traditional Korean outfit

and the period of rapid development that followed, though they have seen a revival in recent decades.

Embroidery and knot art

It wasn't only painting that thrived in the Joseon era. Women let their artistry soar through the delicate process of embroidery (*jasu*) and decorative knot craft (*maedeupjang*). Everyday objects were embroidered, and these items were full of propitious Chinese symbols such as butterflies (signifying domestic happiness).

The best embroiderers in the land were employed by the royal Joseon court, which had its own embroidery department. The ranks of officials were indicated through embroidered panels on their outfits, with civil servants distinguished by crane (and other bird) patterns, the king by a dragon and the queen by a phoenix.

Decorative knots have traditionally been attached to pieces of embroidery

Above Decorative tassel adorning a musical instrument

Below Rows of ceramic pots

Right *Electronic Superhighway* (1995) by Nam June Paik

or to musical instruments and other items. Practitioners use a silk string to make a complex knot, complete with a tassel. Today, Korean decorative knots and embroidered patches commonly adorn hanbok (traditional Korean outfits) worn on special occasions.

Masterful ceramics

While embroidery holds a special place in the history of Korean art, the height of the country's artistic output is arguably ceramics. Korea is covered in lofty granite mountains, and the sediment that accrues from these peaks has helped to form a ready supply of clay, with the oldest pottery found in Korea dating to around 6000 BCE. While these prehistoric vessels were formed over open pits, ceramics made during the Three Kingdoms period benefited from imported Chinese techniques, namely potters' wheels and kiln firing. The pinnacle of Korean ceramics is Goryeo celadon (or *cheongja*), which gets its subdued greenish-blue hue through iron in the clay and other chemical compounds in the glaze. By the 1100s, the master potters of Goryeo were moving beyond Chinese influences, using inlay techniques that involved etching designs into the clay, filling the concavities with slip and then applying glaze. Huge hauls of Goryeo celadon bound for the Silk Road have been recovered from shipwrecks since the 1970s, highlighting the might of the industry.

The pottery of Korea's next and final dynasty, Joseon, was primarily white, hence the term *baekja* (white

porcelain). The simplicity of *baekja* worked well with the neo-Confucian ideals of the time, which revered a plain aesthetic. Such was the skill of the Joseon-era potters that the two major Japanese invasions of Korea known as the Imjin War (1592-1598) saw thousands of artisans captured and forcibly relocated to Japan. Now commonly known as the pottery wars, these conflicts exacted a painful cultural toll, while the relocated Korean artisans elevated Japanese ceramics to new heights.

Produced through centuries of esteemed craftmanship, Korea's priceless ceramics are now proudly displayed in institutions like the National Museum and the Leeum Museum of Art. Pottery of a humbler sort, meanwhile, is ubiquitious, found in the form of *onggi*, dark clay pots for storing fermented foods like kimchi.

formally on home soil during the period of Japanese occupation (1910-1945), artists often chose to attend institutions like the Tokyo Fine Arts School. The great artist Lee Jung-seob (1916-1956) was educated in Japan, learning techniques he would later use to capture the rural soul of Korea in his oil paintings. The abstract artist Kim Whanki (1913-1974) also learnt his trade in Tokyo, though his early work included Korean touches such as women in hanbok. His style evolved until he settled on minutely detailed rows of blue cell-like dots and lines, and this work laid the path for the *dansaekhwa* (monochrome) movement, which began in the 1970s. Decidedly minimalistic, *dansaekhwa*

Age of transition

Just as Korean ceramics were originally indebted to Chinese influence, other global art forms began pouring into Korea at the end of the 19th century. Oil painting, introduced by Western artists, presented an alternative to ink, which had held sway for hundreds of years. This instigated an era of artistic experimentation, as Korean artists sought to carve out a modern identity, and paved the way for pioneering contemporary visionaries like Nam June Paik (1932-2006).

It wasn't easy for budding Korean artists to make a name for themselves in these new artistic fields, however. Having no opportunities to study

Nam June Paik

Nam June Paik (1932–2006) was the most influential Korean artist of the 20th century. Born in Seoul, Paik fled at the start of the Korean War, ending up in New York. After an early career as an avant-garde composer, Paik began making his trademark sculptural installations featuring televisions. A joker as well as a cerebral artist, Paik has left behind hundreds of works, including large robot-shaped figures made of TVs and a giant TV pagoda.

artists like Park Seo-bo (1931–) tended towards subdued colours and immersed themselves in Buddhist and Taoist philosophy. Since 2000, *dansaekhwa* has seen a comeback, with the art capitals of the world hosting exhibitions featuring artists from both the first and second wave.

Contemporary style

As censorship loosened in the 1980s under the Chun Doo-hwan presidency, greater freedom of expression saw a flourishing of the artistic scene. The febrile political atmosphere played its part too, with the Gwangju Uprising (1980) inspiring countrywide protests for democracy. From this arose *minjung* ("people-gathering") art. Folksy and political, *minjung* art appeared on protest banners and walls as well as canvases. Art as a political weapon returned in the mid-2010s, with former president Park Geun-hye fiercely

Wave (2020), an impressive digital art display in Seoul

satirized by painters like Hong Sung-dam (1955-). For their troubles, such artists ended up on a government blacklist, facing censorship, the withholding of public support and exclusion from cultural events.

Away from politics, a prevailing movement since the mid-2000s has been interdisciplinary media art, featuring genre-bending works that combine performance elements like dance with film. One milestone in Korean media art was *Wave* (2020), a huge public installation in Seoul that made use of two LED displays to create the striking illusion of a wave crashing repeatedly within a rectangular box.

Despite global influences and ever-improving technological media, some currents of Korean art remain in confident harmony with tradition. For one, the photographer Bae Bien-u (1950-), known for his haunting black-and-white views of pine trees and other organic forms, continues the work of landscape contemplation that started with the advent of ink painting.

While a new generation of Korean artists turn to the past to renew the country's cultural heritage, modern creatives turn national identity inside out, exploring it from unexpected angles. With robust government funding and a great abundance of world-class museums and galleries, Korea's artistic flourishing will continue — both within tradition and beyond.

Seminal artistic moments

The course of Korean art history has been shaped by discovery and experimentation. These moments irrevocably changed the artistic scene.

660
The Baekje capital (modern Buyeo) is overrun, with much of the kingdom's artistic legacy destroyed.

1300s
Exquisite water-moon *Avalokiteshvara* paintings on scrolls mark the high point of Korean Buddhist painting.

1816
Painter Kim Hong-do completes his albums of genre paintings, preserving everyday life in Joseon.

1500s
Shin Saimdang (1504–1551) paints her folding screen depicting plants and insects, inspiring embroiderers.

1900
Japanese archaeologists begin digging for Korean artistic treasures, with an eye on Goryeo celadon.

1951
Female painter Chun Kyung-ja (1924–2015) shows *The State of Life*, summing up the wartime zeitgeist.

1998
Artist Nam June Paik meets President Bill Clinton at the White House — and drops his pants.

1995
The Gwangju Biennale, Asia's first biannual festival of contemporary art, makes its debut.

1971
The country's first private art gallery opens, showing artworks gathered by art collector Jeon Hyeong-pil.

벽화 마을

Mural villages

After the Korean War, many poor neighbourhoods formed organically, with poverty-stricken residents staking out spots for makeshift shacks high on barren hillsides. These labyrinthine "moon villages" (daldongne), as they became known because of their high vantage point, were for decades stigmatized and neglected. The government's answer? To bring art and culture to these areas.

The Ihwa neighbourhood in Seoul, at the time facing redevelopment, was one of several neighbourhoods selected for a makeover. Korean artists came from far and wide to decorate the walls of the winding alleyways with colourful art, including a koi fish mural painted on a public stairway. Many of these murals made clever use of angles; the koi, for example, only appeared in its entirety when seen from a specific spot. The initiative was a success, bringing in many businesses and tourists.

For the government, murals were found to be effective at revitalizing communities, both economically and culturally, and the strategy was employed all over the country. The lauded walls of Busan's Gamcheon Culture Village were decorated by artists, students and residents themselves. For some residents, however, the increase in foot traffic, noise levels and inevitable gentrification are real issues, with some residents painting over the famed koi mural in Ihwa as an act of resistance.

Giant fish mural in Ihwa Mural Village, painted over in 2016

Architectural lineage

From rustic farmhouses to avant-garde monoliths, Korea's varied architectural aesthetics reflect the country's history, values and ambitions.

Over the centuries, Koreans have adapted their architecture to suit different institutions and objectives, from the early reverence for natural simplicity to the modern obsession with speed and utility. While rapid modernization ruptured the simple practices of traditional construction, the country now strives to integrate the wisdom of its architectural past.

Traditional aesthetics

Traditionally, buildings both high (royal palaces, mountain temples) and low (merchants' shops, farmhouses) eschewed extremes. Instead, builders sought harmony with nature through the use of natural materials, like stone and wood, and understated features like gently sloping roofs.

This approach can be seen in *hanok*, traditional Korean homes. Stone provides the building's base, and timber – usually pine – is used to build the frame and floor. Walls are a mixture of straw and packed earth, often a red clay called *hwangto*. The slatted wooden doors and windows are covered with treated mulberry paper (*hanji*) that's both breathable and water-resistant. Roofs are formed from tiles or rice-straw thatch. The beauty of these readily available components is that they can be easily pulled down and reused to build new structures.

The close connection between *hanok* and the natural world extends to their shape and floorplan. In the north, *hanok* were customarily built in a rectangle around a small courtyard to keep out cold winds. In the south, where winters are mild, they were constructed in a straight line to maximize airflow. Regardless of their shape, all *hanok* generally incorporate a *madang* (courtyard) and an

ingenious underfloor heating system called *ondol*.

The Korean War and, later, the rush to modernize destroyed many traditional buildings; Seoul alone had an estimated 129,000 *hanok* in 1961 but less than 12,000 by the mid-2010s. In recent years, though, these structures have found a renewed appeal. Many have been converted into cafés and restaurants, and Seoul has built an entirely new neighbourhood of *hanok*. Builders are also merging past and present, constructing *sinhanok*, or "new *hanok*", with traditional and sustainable frameworks but strikingly modernized interiors.

Decorative colouring on the rafters and beams of a traditional building, Jeonju

Contemporary utility

The buildings that began to replace traditional *hanok* throughout the 20th century represented a steady change in Korean architecture, catalyzed by events both at home and abroad. As the nation gradually opened to the outside world, foreign architectural styles arrived, a trend that accelerated during the Japanese occupation. Later, the destruction of towns and villages during the Korean War resulted in a frenzied rush to rebuild and redevelop, with speed prized above all else. Global designs became prominent as Korea looked to the outside world to inspire its large-scale urban restoration.

Governments and construction firms responded to the country's booming population and urbanization with a pragmatic shift to a range of new designs and materials. Wood, stone and clay gave way to concrete and brick. Small apartment structures and three- or four-story buildings divided into flats replaced *hanok* as the typical Korean residence; beginning in the 1970s, these in turn were steadily replaced by modern apartment tower complexes, particularly in urban neighbourhoods.

At the same time, influential architects like Kim Swoo-geun (1931–1986) fomented a modern Korean aesthetic, adapting tradition to contemporary architecture. One of the first structures to do this successfully was Seoul Olympic Stadium, which Kim designed for the 1988 Summer Games, with lines that imitated the graceful curves of a Joseon-era porcelain vase.

Learning from the past

Since the turn of the millennium, this fusion of past and present, domestic and international has become the rule, rather than the exception. Many new structures incorporate traditional elements. This can be as simple as a sleek office building with an interior patio inspired by *madang* or as ostentatious as Seoul's Lotte World Tower, which is designed to evoke a calligraphy brush and, at 555 m (1,820 ft), is the tallest building in the country. Architects, development companies and the government are also placing a renewed emphasis on

sustainability and natural resources in building design. Perhaps the most dramatic example is Songdo International Business District, a city built entirely from scratch on 600 ha (1,500 acres) of reclaimed land. It has the highest concentration of LEED-certified projects in the world, a guarantee of its sustainable materials and design.

The lineage of Korean architecture tells a fascinating story, with structures responding to a shifting array of social needs and trends. The result is a national aesthetic that speaks eloquently of the forces that shaped the modern nation.

Ondol

One of Korean architecture's most unusual features is a system of underfloor heating known as *ondol*. The basic design dates back at least two millennia, with flues connected to a kitchen's fireplace. The flues direct its heat and smoke beneath the home's floorboards, warming the house and, incidentally, keeping rats and other pests away. The flues' careful construction keeps smoke from quickly escaping, ensuring that the home remains cosy.

1 Gyeongbokgung Palace

2 Separate complexes at Tongdosa Temple

3 A *hanok* in Jeonju Hanok Village

4 The walls of Hwaseong Fortress

5 Zaha Hadid's Dongdaemun Design Plaza

Though Korean architecture comprises an array of influences and styles, there are a number of important designs that stand out over the centuries.

Palaces

Nearly all the royal structures in Korea date to the Joseon era (1392–1910). Such buildings were exalted versions of traditional architecture: think stone bases, wood frames, tile roofs. Their harmonious placement was dictated by *pungsu*, Korean geomancy. Shining examples include Changdeokgung (the layout of which cleverly follows the land's natural contours) and Gyeongbokgung palaces.

Temples and shrines

Buddhist temples and shrines are grander than secular structures, reflecting the religion's importance in Korea. Their elevated significance is revealed in their decoration, most notably *dancheong*, vivid floral and geometric patterns in the five symbolic colours of blue, red, yellow, white and black (*p144*). During the Confucian Joseon dynasty, Buddhism was repressed and most temples were built in the mountains, meaning that many complexes have irregular layouts, depending on topography.

Fortresses

Most fortresses are *sanseong*, or mountain fortresses. Built primarily with stone, they made use of the natural defences provided by the country's rugged landscape. Korean fortress design reached its apex at Hwaseong, built between 1794 and 1796 in Suwon. The fortress's walls, consisting of stone blocks, extend for 5.7 km (3.5 miles), following the ridges of Mount Paldal. Typical of Korean fortresses, Hwaseong had a main gate at each of the four cardinal directions, and beacon towers, where fires enabled communication with nearby fortresses and military facilities.

Hanok

Korea's vernacular architecture is defined by *hanok*. These homes were constructed in both urban and rural locales and were built almost entirely from natural, readily available materials. As every household produced its own kimchi and fermented sauces in the past, *hanok* traditionally featured a platform called a *jangdokdae* at the rear of the house, where kimchi, soy sauce, gochujang and *doenjang* (fermented soybean paste) were stored in jars.

Modern buildings

Today's structures come in two distinct forms. One is largely utilitarian, comprising office towers and apartments. The other is more flamboyant, and seeks to confirm Korea's place as a global economic and creative power. Some statement buildings integrate with the land, like Dominique Perrault's steel and glass valley at Ewha Womans University; others look to stand out as much as possible, such as Zaha Hadid's otherworldly Dongdaemun Design Plaza.

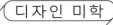

디 자 인 미 학

Design aesthetics

A relative newcomer to the Korean language, the word design — or the English loanword *dijain* — now infiltrates all areas of life. Design has become a thriving industry in and of itself.

An unthinkable luxury when war-torn Korea was first industrializing, design has become central to many aspects of Korean life. Like so much else, good design has become a way of expressing the Korean story and identity, of asserting autonomy and expertise beyond its borders.

Design encompasses myriad forms, from typography to public infrastructure, resulting in a rich but no less cohesive Korean aesthetic. What you see on a graphic poster might influence the blueprints for the latest gadgets. The sweeping curves and smooth surfaces of consumer electronics, meanwhile, are echoed in the nation's well-designed public spaces and ordered interiors.

Graphic identity

When one thinks of design, it's often the graphic kind that comes to mind – something that Korea has been experimenting with for over a century. Korean graphic design began in 1893 with the *Taegeukgi*, the national flag that now represents the Republic of Korea. It's full of symbols *(p144)* that stand for the nation's values, and its predominant use of white symbolizes a desire for peace. The power of graphic design for the nation is equally visible in the official poster for the 1988 Summer Olympics. While the poster bore traces of Japanese style (whose robust visual culture continued to influence Korea's long after the end of the colonial era), it's blend of blue and orange symbolizes

뉴 트 로
Newtro

A trend across design and culture, newtro merges "new" and "retro" for a modern yet vintage look.

SEOUL
1988
SEP.17–OCT.2

제24회 서울올림픽대회
JEUX DE LA XXIVEME OLYMPIADE

Graphic designers

Korea has a thriving design scene, and many innovators are reshaping the field with their pioneering graphics.

Ahn Sang-soo

A leading typographic designer, Ahn Sang-soo creates typefaces inspired by *Hangeul* letter forms.

Seehee Chae

Seehee Chae's colourful illustrations have been seen on credit cards and album covers. She also created illustrations for Team Korea at the FIFA Women's World Cup™.

Sulki and Min

Choi Sulki and Choi Sung Min partner with numerous cultural institutions around the world to create striking promos and designs.

Hong and Kim

Eunjoo Hong and Hyungjai Kim run G& Press, which publishes distinctive graphic design books and zines.

lighting, with identifiably Korean ones, like silk-screen room dividers and low-to-the-ground furniture. Most middle-class homes and office spaces are also fundamentally practical, with consumer technology working alongside more rustic comforts.

Korea's moniker, the Land of the Morning Calm.

Going hand-in-hand with graphic design, typography has also played its part in Korea's visual identity. Few aspects of classical culture inspire as much pride as *Hangeul*, developed in 1443 as an easily learned alternative to Chinese ideograms. And *Hangeul*'s typography has changed little over the centuries. Since the advent of desktop publishing in the 1980s, the clean-lined, clustered letterforms of *Hangeul* – recognizable at a glance even to those unable to read it – have come in an ever wider variety of typefaces. Some of these evoke the hand-painted signs of Korea's past, while others adopt the look and feel of its digital present.

Curated interiors

Of course, design isn't just restricted to posters and prints – it permeates everyday life too. Whether domestic or commercial, many spaces in Korea are by necessity modest in scale and basic layout. It falls to interior design (referred to simply using the loan-word *interieo*) to imbue them with personality. Many use distinctive combinations of Western trends, such as leather sofas and track

Smart products

It's not just the space of the home itself that benefits from striking design, but the products found within. For consumer electronic companies like LG, the external design of a device is just as vital as the cutting-edge technology that's found within. LG envisions its range of TVs sitting upon the wall like framed artwork, using ultra-slim designs to complement the space. It's now introduced the first

Obangsaek

Traditional Korean design features the *Obangsaek* colour spectrum. The five colours each represent an orientation and one of the five elements: blue for east/wood; red for south/fire; yellow for centre/earth; white for west/metal; and black for north/water. *Obangsaek* relates to the theory of yin and yang, which highlights the need for a balanced life. These ideas are encapsulated by the Korean national flag, the *Taegeukgi*, which features the *taegeuk*, or yin-yang symbol, and makes use of four of the five cardinal colours.

"rollable" TV, which folds up almost like wallpaper, to become entirely inconspicuous when not in use.

Public infrastructure

This detail-oriented ethos also applies to the country's well-designed public spaces. The spirit that produced the Seoul Olympic Park in Gangnam has continued into the 21st century, and its best-known example is the Cheonggyecheon, a nearly 11-km (7-mile) stream running through downtown Seoul. Built over an old highway, the new development marked a shift from the concrete-pouring mindset of the mid-20th century to one of urban restoration.

This exhilarating wave of high-design development extends to the islands in the Han River, including Nodeul Island, with its elaborate complex of spaces dedicated to art, music and other cultural pursuits. This lively and distinctive design has become a hallmark of modern Korean culture, and a key means by which the country carves out its singular identity.

Left The *Taegeukgi*, featuring the *Obangsaek* colours

Below The Cheonggyecheon, central Seoul

Stocked shelves
at Blue Square
Book Park in Seoul

KOREA IS
**TELLING
STORIES**

The literary canon

Koreans might spend more time online today, but the appetite for reading remains strong, with literature shining a light on the issues that are driving and defining society.

When Han Kang's *The Vegetarian* won the Man Booker International Prize in 2016, the world was bowled over by Korean literature – just as it has been by K-everything. But poets and novelists have long been providing bedtime stories for Koreans, and today, new writers are joining the global greats at a faster clip than ever.

Folklore and fables

The oldest form of Korean story-telling is the legends, shamanic myths and folktales that have been passed down orally for generations. Folktales in particular functioned like fables, and the purpose of these stories was as varied as the methods used to tell them. Some marked the passing of the seasons and were told around a fire; others recounted social tragedies, and were performed as *pansori* (lyrical storytelling). Important lessons were ingrained in the fabric of these tales, and the emphasis on moral instruction carried through to the first works written and printed in *Hangeul*.

Vernacular literature

The birth of *Hangeul* in 1443 *(p34)* opened up new prospects for vernacular literature. The first *Hangeul* poem – *Yongbieocheonga* (Song of the Dragons Flying to Heaven) – was published in 1447 and documented the changing fortunes of the Joseon dynasty. Just as the earliest oral tales were concerned with spiritual belief, the poem charts the rise of Confucian and Buddhist virtues, and celebrates Korea's moral and spiritual fortitude.

As the audience for vernacular writing grew, literature expanded beyond its spiritual origins. One of the first fictional works to achieve huge popularity was the 18th-century

147

Iconic literature

The Cloud Dream of the Nine

One of the first Korean works to be translated into English, Kim Man-jung's multi-layered 1687 master-piece is infused with Buddhist and Confucian ideas.

Yi Sang: Selected Works

Yi Sang's (1910–1937) avant-garde short stories and poems are experimental and tinged with melancholy.

Youth, It's Painful

An entire generation was inspired by this 2011 collection of essays by Seoul National University professor Kim Rando.

Reasons for Travel

Kim Young-ha's book of essays on travel hit a chord with Koreans when published in 2019.

Misaeng

A nine-part graphic novel series published between 2012 and 2013, *Misaeng* is about the travails of a low-ranking office worker.

novel *The Biography of Hong Gildong*. Its impact was twofold: it harnessed the tropes of old Korean fables to narrate the journey of its protagonist, while questioning the changing fortunes of the modern nation.

State of the nation

Beyond folktales, another significant genre in the Korean canon is political commentary – no surprise, given the huge impact that both Japanese occupation and the Korean War had on the population. Fundamentally,

Below Young writers: Yi Sang, novelist Park Tae Won and poet Kim So-un, around 1936

Left Kim Jiyoung, Born 1982 book cover

The Biography of Hong Gildong showed how writers could use the trappings of traditional storytelling to ask political questions – a tool that was embraced by a new generation of writers by the 20th century. Keen to create a distinct style of Korean literature, written in *Hangeul*, and focus on present-day concerns were innovative writers like Yi Sang and Yi Kwang-su. Yi Kwang-su's *The Heartless* (1917) is a fine example of this new style; often cited as Korea's first modern novel, it captures the speech of regular folk, and follows a love triangle set against the backdrop of Japanese occupation.

Works that reflected the issues of the time held a powerful place in the literary canon. That often meant themes of exile and social breakdown, as in the bleak novella *An Aimless Bullet* (1959), which details the alienation and destitution felt by refugees who resettled after the Korean War.

Modern voices

Political writing has long been dominated by male voices, but a wellspring of powerful feminist fiction written by and about women has flourished in the last decade. In 2016, Cho Nam-Joo released *Kim Jiyoung, Born 1982* – a powerful story about a woman's psychosis in the face of misogyny. However, this story made such an impact that some men targeted supporters of the book and vented about its content online. Despite Korea's enduring patriarchal society, feminist writers continue to use fiction to speak freely about gendered issues, including domestic

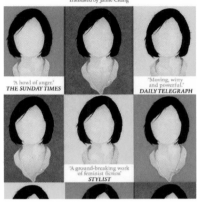

KIM JIYOUNG, BORN 1982

CHO NAM-JOO

Translated by Jamie Chang

'A howl of anger.'
THE SUNDAY TIMES

'Moving, witty and powerful.'
DAILY TELEGRAPH

'A ground-breaking work of feminist fiction'
STYLIST

violence, professional inequality and damaging beauty standards.

Literature might still be used to make political statements, but the books topping the charts today tend to mark a move away from politics to escapism and education. Popular non-fiction topics include self-help, education, finance and travel, reflecting a culture where personal growth is paramount.

The power of social media and TV has also done wonders for Korean stories. Take *Pachinko* (2017) by Korean American author Min Jin Lee. First written in English, the book follows a Korean family who immigrates to Japan. Its popularity in the US saw interest surge in Korea, with the book translated into Korean and adapted into a series by Apple TV+, increasing its sales. Alongside the loud appeal of K-pop and K-drama, Korean stories and books continue to exert a quiet influence, challenging and enthralling new readers around the world.

번역의 기술

The art of translation

Translating the literature of any language is a tricky proposition, but Korean is especially so. For one, Korean has many forms of politeness and terms of address *(p36)*, like *sieomeoni* ("mother-in-law", but only when spoken by a woman). Translate this literally and it sounds clunky; use a natural-sounding word in the target language, and something is lost.

Adding to the problem is the lateness with which Korea – closed to the wider world as it was for centuries – came to the translation scene. It wasn't until the 1980s that its literary works became more widely available overseas and domestically in other languages. Government involvement helped in the 1990s with the founding of the Literature Translation Institute of Korea; today, the LTI Korea provides translation grants for Korean literature. But there's much more work to be done. While Deborah Smith's translation of Han Kang's *The Vegetarian* in 2015 propelled the book to global acclaim, many academics criticized Smith's work as not being literal enough. And it's not just literature that raises translation concerns. When K-drama *Squid Game* was released in 2021, the English subtitles drew controversy, with many claiming that the translations "botched" the intended meaning – the most important aspect of any story. Yet, with Korean culture becoming more widely known – take Bora Chung's *Cursed Bunny*, which was shortlisted for the International Booker Prize in 2022 – the hope is that less will be lost and much more gained in translations.

Bora Chung, author of *Cursed Bunny*

Fashion focus

Globally recognized for their sartorial choices, Koreans have diversified their wardrobes since the days of traditional hanbok, and bold clothing is now a marker of style and autonomy.

While Korean fashion is today known for its self-expression, the idea of using clothing to show individuality is relatively new. Since Western fashion was introduced in the 20th century, trends have evolved with remarkable speed, reflecting the global outlook of a country at the forefront of modern innovation. However, the clean-cut lines and muted colours of old remain central expressions of Korean heritage.

Modest origins

Traditional clothing was defined by the elegant uniformity of the hanbok. Hanbok literally means "Korean clothing", but refers specifically to the garments worn from the Three Kingdoms period (57 BCE–668 CE) onwards. While there have been variations, early hanbok consisted

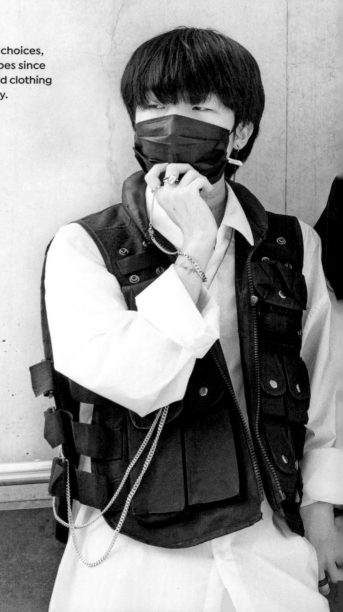

Street style on display
during Seoul Fashion
Week, 2022

of a *jeogori* (a top tied together
with string), a *chima* (skirt) and *baji*
(trousers). While wealthier Koreans
wore embroidered hanbok made of
a fabric called ramie, most people
made do with plain, white cotton. When
Japanese colonists interpreted the
wearing of white as a symbol of resistance,
Koreans continued to sport white hanbok
to protest occupation (many referred
to themselves as *baegui minjok,* or the
"people clothed in white").

As Western styles became prevalent
and Korea looked beyond its borders in
the latter half of the 20th century, there
were concerns that hanbok would be
forgotten. To combat this, in 1996 the
government designated 21 October as
National Hanbok Day. Since then, hanbok
with shorter skirts and modern patterns
by designers like Lee Young-hee have
flourished, while older hanbok are still
worn during weddings and holidays.

Style evolution

Simple clothing still dominated
after World War II, when a focus on
economic recovery meant flamboyance
was equated with needless expense.
However, a higher GDP and exposure
to new global fashion through colour
TV broadened style sensibilities
in the 1980s. The Seoul Olympics
in 1988 then saw a proliferation of
tourists bringing new global styles
into the country. Designer items worn
by celebrities became aspirations,
and bright athletic wear from brands
like Nike swept the nation. Youths
began to rebel against their parents'
thrifty philosophies, accessorizing
mandatory school uniforms with
the latest trainers and backpacks.

An explosion of vibrant street style
followed in the 1990s. Gangnam in
Seoul became the nucleus, with
the so-called "Orange Tribe" *(Orenji-
jok)* – a group of wealthy students
influenced by foreign brands and
the proliferation of pop culture –
promoting an array of luxury styles
from both the US and Japan.

Today, Seoul Fashion Week
has become one of Asia's most
anticipated events, with forward-
thinking designers synthesizing global
styles and traditional designs. In a
society of such rapid modernization,
even the keenest observer might
struggle to keep up with the dizzying
evolution of Korean fashion.

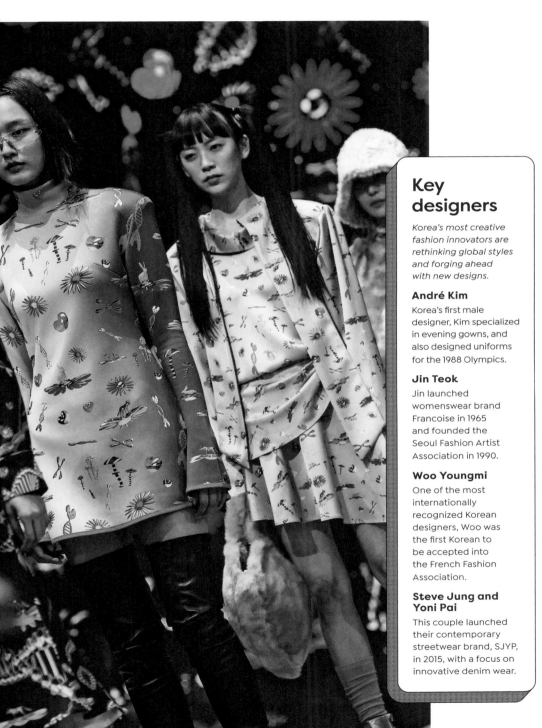

Key designers

Korea's most creative fashion innovators are rethinking global styles and forging ahead with new designs.

André Kim

Korea's first male designer, Kim specialized in evening gowns, and also designed uniforms for the 1988 Olympics.

Jin Teok

Jin launched womenswear brand Francoise in 1965 and founded the Seoul Fashion Artist Association in 1990.

Woo Youngmi

One of the most internationally recognized Korean designers, Woo was the first Korean to be accepted into the French Fashion Association.

Steve Jung and Yoni Pai

This couple launched their contemporary streetwear brand, SJYP, in 2015, with a focus on innovative denim wear.

Performing a *talchum*
(mask dance) in
Andong City

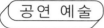

Performing arts

Performance is in Korea's blood. Before the written word, drama and opera were a means for self-expression and swapping stories, and their power endures today.

While everyone seems excited about the latest thing in Korea, the performing arts world has been quietly ensuring that ancient stories and traditions are kept alive. From comedic mask dance dramas to impassioned *pansori* (lyrical storytelling) performances, the performing arts scene is utterly captivating.

Behind the mask

Korean theatre has its roots in *talchum* – mask dance dramas, where performers tell stories with movement, not words. The focus is on dancing, singing, miming and performing acrobatics, which, along with magnificent costumes,

progress the narrative. The form emerged as shamanic ritual, and was believed to dispel bad sprits and misfortunes, but as civilization grew, so did *talchum*. During the Joseon period, masks were seen less as sacred objects and more as a form of expression and entertainment. *Namsadang* – travelling troupes of the lowest class men – would wander around villages and perform their mask dramas in the open-air for the working classes, especially during festivals and national holidays.

Beyond the impressive costumes and infectious dances, *talchum* was so entertaining for the masses because it often mocked the

privileged upper class, and could get away with doing so through comedy and the safety of a mask. Though each mask dance drama varies by region and performer, they all share key characteristics: obscenity, satire and ridicule. Exaggerated masks are worn to represent different characters – including gods, shamans, corrupted noblemen and animals – and make political statements, while humour is used as a way of making light of quite serious subjects. Often in the firing line are patriarchal husbands and apostate monks; a popular theme involves a monk who is tempted by a young woman and forgets his duties, only to be berated by the woman's lover, who criticizes his depravity and chases him away.

창극
Changgeuk
A traditional Korean opera performed as a play with a large cast, in contrast to *pansori*.

Operatic tendencies

While *talchum* leans towards the humorous, *pansori* is more dramatic, even tragic. Akin to Western opera, *pansori* is performed by a solo singer (often a woman) and a drummer (often a man), and emphasizes the beauty of the Korean language through impressive vocal techniques and lyrics.

The form is believed to have originated in the 17th-century Joseon era, when it was likely performed to the lower classes by shamans and street artists. By the mid-18th century, the upper classes and royal families started embracing the form, causing it to become more elitist. While it moved behind closed doors as a form of court entertainment, *pansori* didn't shy away from sharing the stories of working class struggles, speaking for voices otherwise unheard by the nobility.

Five *pansori* tales are still widely performed today: *Chunhyangga, Simcheongga, Heungbuga, Sugungga* and *Jeokbyeokga*. Of these tales, it's *Chunhyangga* – a heartfelt story of

two lovers – that's arguably the most memorable. It's a story that's survived through the ages, stunningly retold and reimagined by numerous companies; the Korean ballet company Universal Ballet has been performing *The Love of Chunhyang* since 2007.

A feat of endurance

It's a testament to the stories told through *pansori* and *talchum* that the forms have managed to endure. Both on the UNESCO Intangible Cultural Heritage list today, they survive even as new stories enter the fold, whether it's a reinventing of *pansori* (as in the case of pop songs by fusion band Leenalchi) or the introduction of an avant-garde theatre scene. At their very core, *pansori* and *talchum* were made to entertain – something that will no doubt ensure their popularity for centuries to come.

Left A figure dressed as a lion during a *talchum* performance

Above A *pansori* performance, Jeonju

Popular pansori tales

Chunhyangga
The love story of Chunhyang, the daughter of a *gisaeng* (female entertainer), and Mong-ryong, the son of a nobleman, is often regarded as the best *pansori*.

Simcheongga
A tragic *pansori*, this tale deals with a woman's struggles to help her blind father regain his sight.

Heungbuga
This humorous folksy tale focuses on the struggle between a good and evil brother.

Sugungga
A frank satire, this *pansori* looks at the relationship of subject and king through the personification of a hare in a sea kingdom.

Jeokbyeokga
A retelling of the heroic historical legend of the Chinese Battle of Red Cliffs (208–209 CE), this *pansori* is said to be the most difficult to sing.

KOREA IS
ENTERTAINING THE WORLD

BTS, *Parasite*, *Squid Game*: these household names are responsible for getting the world hooked on Korean culture. But how did South Korea – a country that was formed not even a century ago by a tumultuous split across the peninsula – become a global trendsetter? There's no simple answer, but in the intentional pursuit of soft power in the 1990s, Korea's government found a way to commoditize its culture. And Korea has gradually expanded its influence beyond its borders ever since, entertaining fans worldwide with K-everything. It's noticeably paid off (and it pays well, too, with K-pop alone a billion-dollar industry). The transformation has been nothing short of phenomenal, with K-pop and K-drama securing adoring fanbases and directors and actors sweeping awards ceremonies – no doubt just the start of what Korea can achieve.

(음악 장르)

Music styles

Beyond headline-hogging K-pop is a rich repertoire of folk anthems, power ballads and indie rock classics, all ready to make the playlist.

Whether it's a soft warble coming from a trot singer or a soulful riff played by a rock guitarist, Korea's musicians inspire and entertain in equal measure. An assortment of styles make up the country's musical landscape, ranging from deeply traditional to playfully experimental.

Tracing traditions

Korea's musical canon begins with *gugak*: national music that tends to encompass both court and folk music. While music has been around since the prehistoric times, the term

gugak only arose in the Joseon era, marking the period when Korea fully embraced music for the first time. Helping matters was the creation of Korea's own musical notation system in 1447; with music easier than ever to compose, it fast became a beloved form of court entertainment. Of the various *gugak* genres, *jeongak* (classical music, which features an ensemble of traditional wind, string, and percussion instruments) and *pansori* (lyrical storytelling) were by far the most common.

Six centuries on, *gugak* still has its place, though has undergone reinventions. In the last decade, a new generation of crossover pop and *gugak* artists such as sEODo and Agust D have revived interest in the art form, particularly among younger people. TV producers have furthered this revival, with the popular competitive TV show *Poongryu – Battle Between Vocalists* airing in 2021.

Below Playing the bamboo flute, *daegeum*

Right Member of sEODo Band, which combines Joseon era music with pop

Arirang

Considered Korea's unofficial anthem, this folk song has been around in both North and South Korea for more than six centuries. Passed down by memory through the generations, *Arirang* is thought to have around 3,600 variations. The song became a resistance anthem during Japanese rule, and it's also sung to express loss and hope for a country divided. Today, it's inscribed on UNESCO's Intangible Cultural Heritage of Humanity list.

Hot to trot

Korea's original form of pop music isn't K-pop *(p166)* – it's trot. Developed in the 20th century during Japanese rule, trot derives from "foxtrot", and became influenced by American, European and Japanese musical styles over the decades. Also known by the onomatopoeic term *ppongjjak*, after the simple two-beat rhythm, trot has a simple melody, which listeners can sing along to with ease. Themes are traditionally centred around love, loss and separation, perhaps between lovers or the North and South peninsula. But for all their emotional resonance, trot songs can also be fun and upbeat, with light-hearted lyrics.

Though it was Korea's most popular genre from the 1960s to the early 80s, trot fell out of favour in the 1990s. Primarily, its melancholic lyrics and trademark *kkeokk-ki* singing style – where the singer bends and flexes their voice – were pushed out by the shiny new K-pop genre. But there was another reason: trot also drew scorn for having its roots in Japanese *enka* music, a stinging reminder of the occupation.

Despite its ups and downs, trot has managed to retain its popularity

through the decades. Today, a new set of artists – as well as the ubiquitous competitive singing shows, in this case *Miss Trot* and *Mr. Trot* – are keeping it fresh.

The power of the ballad

Audiences may shape what's popular, but so does the government. During the 1980s, censorship rules banned any kind of provocative content; as a result, music shows, long on TV screens, stuck primarily to airing soft, saccharine, love-lorn ballads, as well as trot music.

Power ballads and sentimental love songs remain one of the country's most enduring genres. They form the soundtracks to romantic K-dramas, be it *Guardian: The Lonely and Great God* (2016) or *Descendants of the Sun* (2016), and fill *noraebang* (singing rooms) across the country. Ballad songwriters are particularly deft at taking listeners on an emotional arc through expressive melodies and lyrical sensitivity. The best vocalists are masterful at soul-stirring performances, shifting between soft, delicate warbles and soaring dramatic crescendos. Done well, singers draw tears from rapt listeners and provide catharsis by the end.

Cradle of indie

For every power-ballad warbler or bubblegum pop star, there's an indie alternative waiting. In the

1990s, while K-pop idols were being trained to enter the mainstream charts, an underground punk community was forming in Hongdae, the creative cradle of Seoul. For audiences seeking the opposite of commercialized, highly processed pop tunes and shiny stars moulded to perfection, such counterculture was ideal. And it wasn't just punk rock; folk, rap and grunge contributed to the indie scene, too.

Today, everything from acoustic to lo-fi lounge, rock to folk, falls under the "K-indie" category. And though indie usually reaches a niche audience by definition, a growing number of Korean artists have found mainstream success. Indie band Hyukoh's EP *22* made it into the Top 10 of the Billboard World Albums Chart in 2015, and

Busker Busker's 2012 song "Cherry Blossom Ending" (which re-enters the charts every spring) was named Korea's best-selling single ever in 2021. But this fame doesn't compromise the integrity of the scene; K-indie is, at its core, artist-driven, with success seen as organic rather than engineered.

Feel the music

Ultimately, Korean music is not just a mode of entertainment but of storytelling – of heartache and longing, of raging against the system, or acknowledging rich histories. Whether they're creating modern renditions of *gugak*, trot or ballads, crafting an alternative soundtrack or catapulting K-pop into the global charts, Korea's musicians are a force to be reckoned with.

Left Indie group Busker Busker performing in Seoul

Right Lee Sun-hee, one of Korea's top ballad singers

Musical legends

Lee Mi-ja
Considered one of the most influential trot singers in Korean history, Lee released 560 albums throughout her 60-year career, which started in 1959.

Shin Jung-hyeon
A guitarist and singer-songwriter, Shin is often described as the "godfather of rock", having formed Korea's first rock band in 1962.

Cho Yong-pil
Many refer to Cho as *Gawang*, or the "singing king". Though he debuted in a rock band in 1968, his solo career has had a huge impact on the pop scene.

Lee Sun-hee
Described as Korea's national diva, Lee shot to fame after winning a TV singing competition in 1984. Her career as a balladeer spans 30 years.

Shin Seung-hun
Known as the "king of ballads", Shin debuted in the 1990s and was the first Korean artist to sell one million albums in the country.

A K-pop powerhouse

A global phenomenon, K-pop has reached every continent on earth and broken innumerable records along the way.

BTS at the American Music Awards, 2021

The well-produced melodies are addictive, the synchronized choreography is honed to perfection, and the adoration for groups like BTS and BLACKPINK is astronomical. This isn't simply pop music. This is K-pop.

More than a genre

What, exactly, makes K-pop different from pop? Both are centred around bubblegum sounds, stylish singers and upbeat dance moves. But K-pop dials things up a notch. This is music to be enjoyed visually as much as heard. Every song is accompanied by intricate choreography, vibrant fashion choices that instantly set trends and immense sets that turn every music video into a film. The songs are carefully constructed, too, a skilful fusion of hip-hop, R'n'B, rock, rap and EDM, as well as different languages. Indeed, fans don't bat an eyelid when a song moves from Korean to English in mere seconds.

Perhaps most importantly, K-pop is about the performers behind the song – so much so that in Korea, the genre isn't known as K-pop, but "idol groups". Here, years are spent creating stars through a highly specific process in which potential idols are scouted, trained and carefully assembled into polished bands. What does it take to get to the top? In the words of BTS's iconic song – some blood, sweat and tears.

The origins of a sensation

With the ushering in of a democratic government in 1987, Korean music underwent a seismic shift. Since broadcasting was no longer under intense state control, Western-style

애교

Aegyo

A cute display of affection. Idols often adopt aegyo, such as using a cute voice or making a heart symbol with their hands, for fans.

music could reach Korea, paving the way for hip-hop band Seo Taiji and Boys to perform a rap-rock break-up song on a television talent show in 1992. The American-style song, with its blend of Korean and English lyrics and energetic choreography, was new and exciting – and completely failed to impress the judges. Yet the nation was captivated: the band soared to the top of the charts, their ski-wear-inspired style took over the streets and their iconic dance moves were

BLACKPINK
performing at
California's Coachella
Festival in 2019

endlessly imitated. The trajectory of music in Korea was irrevocably changed and K-pop was born.

Making of a star

Some might have seen Seo Taiji and Boys' songs (which aired political frustrations through bold lyrics) as disruptive, but they continued to capture the attention of the public – and the music industry. By the time the band retired in 1996, Korea was the 11th richest country in the world, and music honchos were ready to catapult the sound – and the economy – to the next level.

Record producer Lee Soo-man, who had worked with US artists in the heyday of MTV, was one of the first on the scene, spearheading a new studio, SM Entertainment, in 1996. His mission? To churn out stars who could break into the Korean music scene and beyond. And Soo-man wasn't the only one who saw the potential in this new, globally exportable product; the government's investment in culture after the Asian financial crisis of 1997 did as much for K-pop as Seo Taiji and Boys back in 1992.

Debuting an image

In the late 1990s, three powerhouse music studios – SM, joined by JYP Entertainment and YG Entertainment – formulated a training plan for future K-pop stars. On the agenda: singing, dancing and, crucially, building a bond with future fans. To this day, hundreds of talented youngsters

K-pop's biggest moments

From chart-topping singles to iconic videos, K-pop's journey to global phenomenon is nothing short of remarkable.

1992

Seo Taiji and Boys perform "I Know" on a talent show; it stays at number one in Korea for 17 weeks.

1996

First "idol group" H.O.T debut and become the first pop group to sell one million albums in Korea.

2008

Wonder Girls become the first Korean act to chart in the US Billboard Top 100, with "Nobody" at 76.

2007

Rain is the first idol to perform at the renowned Tokyo Dome in Japan – to a sold-out stadium, no less.

2011

Girls' Generation become the first K-pop group to be signed by a US label, Interscope Records.

2012

PSY's "Gangnam Style" goes viral, and the video becomes the first on YouTube to hit one billion views.

2020

BTS secure their first Grammy nomination in the "Best Pop Duo/Group Performance" category.

2018

First openly gay idol Holland's debut song "Neverland", about having a gay relationship, is released.

2017

BTS become the first Korean act to win a Billboard Music Award and perform at the American Music Awards.

attend global auditions held by
these agencies. The end goal? Being
assembled into a chart-topping group.

A trainee might have all the
components (a good voice, dancing
ability, the "right" look) to become a
star on paper, but if they're to be part
of a successful group, they need to
have a niche within the band and
chemistry with the other members.
Once this intricate balance has been
found and groups are put together (a
process that can take years), they're
given a name, teaser photos and
trailers are released, and they're
presented to an audience through
a showcase. If all goes well, music
videos are posted to YouTube, a fan

base builds and tours are started – all
in a matter of weeks. And it doesn't
stop there. After debut, a group's
schedule and media exposure is
carefully dictated. The band may
often be put on hiatus, with members
working on solo projects in between
group activities or simply disappearing from the public eye, building
anticipation for their eventual
"comeback" as a group.

No signs of stopping

It's safe to say that record producers
like Lee Soo-man (as well as the
Korean government) achieved what
they intended: today, K-pop is a huge
force outside of, as well as within,
Korea. While Seo Taiji and Boys
popularized K-pop at home, the
genre has exploded in Western
markets, first through concerts in
Europe and the US in the early 2000s
(which were televised in Korea as
proof that K-pop was its top export),
then by social media.

In 2012, all over the world, people
obsessively watched PSY's "Gangnam
Style", making it the first YouTube
video to reach a billion views. K-pop's
influence only grew from there. Boy
band BTS became the first Korean
group to hit number one on the
Billboard 100 charts, and BLACKPINK
were the first K-pop band to perform
at acclaimed US festival Coachella.

Band breakdown

Groups are far more successful
than solo singers, partly because
fans love to see relationships
form and grow between the
members. Still, each member
must have their own niche and
image. Positions in groups
include rapper, lead vocalist, sub-
vocalist, dancer, *mangnae* (the
youngest member) or "visual"
(the standout star at the front).

Above Girl band
Secret Number
at a release
showcase

Right On set of *Idol
School*, an 11-week
reality TV show

Today, hitting 100 million views for a new music video is par for the course.

So, where does K-pop go from here? It's proven that music can transcend both language and cultural barriers, but its success has also highlighted long-standing criticisms – particularly for its perceived lack of artistic freedom, taxing training practices, long contracts, strict beauty ideals and the pressure for idols to be squeaky clean. While some criticisms have been met with reform, like JYPE's focus on mental health initiatives, and even the rise of virtual bands like girl group Eternity, many believe there's still a long way to go.

K-팝 팬덤

K-pop fandom

Ear-shattering fan chants, beaming lightsticks, finger hearts shot into the air: fans that worship pop bands are nothing new, but when it comes to K-pop, "for the fans" is the unofficial motto. Wearing all the merchandise, purchasing songs on multiple platforms to help break the global charts and even buying advertising space to celebrate a group's anniversary or new release is a standard way to show appreciation for an idol. After all, fans are key to an idol's success and direction.

In fact, K-pop idols are specifically trained to form a connection with their fans, treat them like an extended family member and extend affirmations of gratitude towards them. Relationships are never one-sided; if a fan shows a finger heart, an idol does one right back as a gesture of affection.

Perhaps the most distinctive feature of fandom culture are *hommas*: "homepage masters" of fan sites who play an active role in marketing idols. But they're no regular fans. These fan site masters have a "bias" – a term used to mark their favourite member of a band, whether it's because they admire their talent or find them attractive. They attend every event or concert to take professional photos of this member, and the images are then shared to their followers online, both to spread the love they have for their chosen idol and to show the world how much talent they possess. *Homma* or not, it's the fans who ensure K-pop remains a billion-dollar industry, one finger heart at a time.

Fans shining phone lights at a PSY concert, Seoul

B-boy Gorilla Crew
members dancing on
their studio rooftop

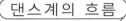

Dance moves

Dance permeates every area of Korea's entertainment scene, but it's not just an accessory to other media – it's an incredible scene within its own right.

Korean dance has been captivating audiences since the earliest kingdoms, when the most popular forms were court, folk and ritual. In these styles, movement is subtle and restrained. Court dances centre around gentle lifts of the feet, shamanistic rituals are all about flowing arm movements and folk styles such as fan dances encourage elegant shapes. And though all styles remain popular, they're worlds away from what's hot today.

A new rhythm

When global influences started pouring into the country by the end of the 20th century, the dance scene was no exception. From the late 1980s to the 1990s, US soldiers and MTV introduced breakdancing and "B-boys" – a form that has since been brought to new heights in Korea. Jinjo Crew, formed in 2001, was the first to win all five major international B-boy competitions by 2012; Laser, a member of Gambler

Crew, is often regarded as the world's best head-spinner; and government-sponsored competitions are ubiquitous. When "breaking" makes its debut as an Olympic sport in 2024, Korea is predicted to sweep up medals.

While breakdancing was taking over the streets at the turn of the century, idols in training were learning intricate moves for each K-pop song. Choreographers are arguably the backbone of the K-pop industry, responsible for turning live shows into theatre and music videos into mini films – a decade on and fans still can't think of PSY's "Gangnam Style" without imitating the video's iconic horse-riding moves.

The 2010s and 20s have witnessed dance enter the TV industry, too. Comical dance scenes make K-drama episodes memorable, and dance variety shows have been increasing, with the likes of *Street Woman Fighter* launching dancers into the limelight. Dance could well be the new K-pop.

Dance styles

Folk
Salpuri is one of the most renowned Joseon-era folk dances. Dancers throw a white scarf into the air to expel evil spirits (*sal* means "negative energy" and *puri* "to release").

Mask dance
Cheoyongmu is a fine example of a Silla-era mask dance *(p156)*. It consists of five dancers whose movements represent symbolic characters.

New dance
Pioneered by idol Choi Seung-hee, this form integrates Korean, Asian and Western dances.

Breakdancing
Influenced by hip-hop crews from the Bronx in New York City, B-boys and B-girls perform imaginative gravity-defying moves.

K-pop cover dance
This global movement sees fans and members of the public produce their own music videos, replicating the dance moves of K-pop songs.

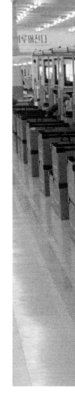

$\boxed{\text{TV 방송 분야}}$

The TV landscape

Despite the proliferation of tablets, laptops and mobile phones for watching YouTube and viral videos, television still makes an impact in Korean households.

Once monitored by military governments between the 1960s and late 80s, the Korean TV industry has come a long way. The first national channel, KBS (Korean Broadcasting System), was born in 1961 – a time when there were only around 300 TV sets in Korea. With the loosening of state controls in the 1990s, the shift towards democracy saw the government invest in both the TV business and electronics. Samsung, for one, had been making televisions since the late 1970s; by the mid-1990s, they'd produced over 20 million colour TVs. With nearly every household in Korea owning a TV by 1995, the industry had an audience ready and waiting.

For a time, national broadcasters had a hold on Korea's TV world, with KBS, MBC (Munhwa Broadcasting Corporation) and SBS (Seoul Broadcasting System) responsible for most TV content, which tended to be news, variety or sports. Major cable channels, such as JTBC, tvN and Mnet, brought more choice from the late 1990s into the 2000s, and wider access to satellite channels from the start of the 21st century sparked interest in

Above A Samsung electronics factory near Seoul, 1985

Left Behind the scenes of a TV show shot during the Seoul Olympics, 1988

US shows. The likes of family friendly *Little House on the Prairie* and *MacGyver* were aired in the 1970s and 80s respectively, but the 2000s introduced shows like *Sex and the City* – much more explicit, by Korea's conservative standards.

Beyond the box

Inevitably, watching habits have evolved with the rise of technology. Much of Korea's digitally connected population view programmes on the go on their mobiles, dipping in and out of shows or watching them in short bursts according to their schedules. There's little need to own a TV set; most people watch shows on the internet through paid subscription services like Wavve. Still, this shift in the mode of consumption hasn't set back the TV business: around 96 per

cent of households own a television set as of 2021. Electronics giants like Samsung and LG continue to dominate TV sales within Korea, and the development of TV technology continues.

Today, streaming platforms and smaller independent studios have taken the lead over terrestrial TV, so much so that they are referred to as OTT (over-the-top media services). Around a third of the population are reported to use foreign streaming giants like Netflix, while about a quarter subscribe to domestic OTT services. The popularity of such platforms arguably stems from their exclusivity, with several K-dramas available only on the likes of Netflix. It's likely, then, that other types of exclusive programming will follow suit in the future to meet the growing preference for streaming services.

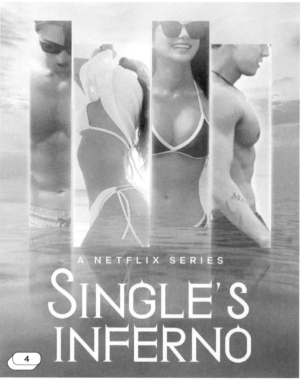

1 Stars of variety
show *Running Man*

2 Netflix's
documentary,
Cyber Hell

3 Kids' favourite,
Baby Shark

4 *Single's Inferno*

WHAT'S ON TV

K-drama *(p180)* might take the title as the country's most enduring genre, but Korea's TV programming is as vast as its audience, with various genres that entertain or educate.

Variety

Arguably the most uniquely Korean of TV genres, variety shows are incredibly diverse in content. They often feature the country's biggest names, from K-pop stars to movie actors, who perform stunts, take part in skits or compete in quizzes to entertain audiences. Laid-back humour and witty banter are a prerequisite for these casual, live shows. Some of the most popular examples include *Running Man* (two teams of celebrities compete in a series of games) and *Men on a Mission* (comedians pretend to be high schoolers in a classroom while celebrity guests stop by for a chat and some games).

Documentaries

Historically, documentaries have been a hugely important platform for reflecting on the country's socio-political climate. Those dating back to the Japanese occupation period and the successive military regimes through the 1980s, for instance, highlighted social injustices and the need for intervention. Themes have expanded to human stories such as the Emmy Award-winning *Mom and the Red Bean Cake* (2010), which traces the life of a single mother with stomach cancer who sells rice cakes. Hard-hitting exposés also have a strong place, like *Cyber Hell: Exposing an Internet Horror* (2022), a Netflix documentary on the country's ongoing digital sex crime crisis.

Children's TV

Korea's children's entertainment industry has made its mark in the 21st century. Among the most sensational hits has been the animated Korean series *Baby Shark's Big Show!* (2020), inspired by the song *Baby Shark*. Though the *Baby Shark* tune has been around since the 20th century (its exact origins are disputed), the song was popularized in Korea in 2016 after Pinkfong – a Korean entertainment company – released a music video version on YouTube, where it went viral. Apart from this huge export, the majority of Korea's youth programming is aired on the Educational Broadcasting System (EBS) network, which offers young ones both education and entertainment shows. Among the most popular Korean cartoon series are *Dooly the Little Dinosaur* and *Pororo the Little Penguin*.

Reality

In the early 2010s, the popularity of US shows like *American Idol* launched a string of similar music competitions in Korea, from *Superstar K* to the *King of Mask Singer*. Dating shows have made their mark, too, with *Single's Inferno* becoming the first Korean reality series to top Netflix's global TV rankings, in 2021. Beyond the contest format, Koreans thrive on documentary-style reality programmes. Popular examples include *My Little Old Boy* and *I Live Alone*, which follows the day-to-day lives of single celebrities living on their own – a response to the growing phenomenon of single-person households.

K-drama influence

Korean dramas may have penetrated the mainstream market at dizzying speeds, but it took clever strategizing, a few key players and some political will to get there.

The breakthrough success of *Squid Game* is nothing short of incredible. This ultra-violent Korean-language show has taken the world by storm, becoming Netflix's most-watched series ever. Not only has this drama introduced new audiences around the world to the ingenuity of Korean TV, it's also showcased the masterful storytelling skills of Korean screen-writers and outstanding performances of the country's top-notch actors. But K-drama doesn't start and end with *Squid Game*.

The making of a genre

Known simply as dramas in Korea, "K-drama" has become a catch-all phrase to describe scripted TV shows. It's used to denote all sorts of genres, be it body-swap rom-coms, sweet coming-of-age stories or scary zombie thrillers. Regardless of the topic, the best K-dramas keep viewers riveted through suspenseful storytelling. Common plot devices include Cinderella makeovers in which dramatic transformations lead to true love, conniving chaebol brought down by their avenging victims and sworn enemies turned lovers.

Typical K-dramas share many characteristics. They usually stretch anywhere between 12 to 24 episodes, end in one season and are led by a

Lee Jung-jae in
the first season of
Squid Game

Popular K-dramas

The World of the Married

The Korean adaptation of the BBC series *Doctor Foster*, this 2020 series is the most-watched cable drama series in Korean television history.

Sky Castle

Hugely popular when it aired in 2018, this black comedy sees wealthy upper-class families competing to get their children into university.

Coffee Prince

This 2007 rom-com made Gong Yoo a breakout star and a global heartthrob.

Boys over Flowers

A classic among early K-drama fans, this 2009 high school drama pits rich against poor.

Jewel in the Palace

Also known as *Dae Jang Geum*, this 2003 historical drama is based on the true story of a young cook who became the king's first female physician during the Joseon dynasty.

Emotions running high in *The World of the Married*

single screenwriter, some of whom boast as much star power and name recognition as the lead actors.

Perhaps one of the biggest features that makes K-dramas distinct is the use of a live-shooting production format, a concept unique to Korean TV. Unlike fully pre-produced shows, in which scripts are written and episodes shot in their entirety before going to air, the live-shoot model lets screenwriters make last-minute changes to scripts and storylines based on show ratings and viewer feedback. If the audience begins to show distaste at the direction of a romantic relationship, or are particularly smitten by a secondary character as the series progresses, the show is rewritten at the last

minute. The whims of audiences are appeased, but for the cast, this often means all-nighters memorizing new lines.

Rising appeal

While K-dramas might seem like a relatively new phenomenon, Korean dramas have been a beloved staple of the country's entertainment industry for decades. In the 1980s and 90s, local broadcasters like KBS, MBC and SBS televised chaste PG-rated rom-coms and family-friendly mini-series that upheld Korean values. When the government began to invest in Korea's cultural capital towards the end of the 20th century, TV dramas were at the forefront. Demand across Asia for Korean productions grew rapidly; not only were these shows a fraction of the cost of those sold out of Japan and Hong Kong, they were also of high production quality.

This demand reached life-changing heights in 2003, when *Winter Sonata* caused a sensation after airing in Japan. Many experts cite this romantic drama as the show that officially launched the Hallyu phenomenon. It turned its lead male actor Bae Yong-joon into an international heartthrob (the Japanese prime minister at the time joked that the actor was more popular than he was), and the show's film location, Nami Island, into a new tourist destination. By the early 2000s, K-drama audiences had grown beyond Asia to the likes of Latin America and the Middle East, the absence of violence, drinking and sex – as well as the emphasis placed on family values – making K-dramas suitable for many conservative countries.

After almost two decades of a somewhat niche following, K-dramas – in tandem with the rise of K-pop and Korean cinema – began to penetrate mainstream Western markets with the arrival of new streaming services. By the late 2000s and into the early 2010s, platforms like Viki (now Rakuten Viki) and DramaFever (now defunct) were streaming K-dramas to global audiences in dozens of languages. These networks, together with the addition of subtitles and dubbing, would boost the mass appeal of K-drama enormously.

A new audience

It wasn't long before streaming giants Netflix, Apple TV+ and Disney+ recognized the global demand for K-content. A key breakthrough for Korean entertainment came in 2019, when Netflix produced its first original K-drama series, *Kingdom*. A historical, supernatural thriller with a big budget attached to it, this new show was written and produced with international audiences in mind. Fast-forward to 2021 and the streaming giant reached new heights, with smash hit *Squid Game* becoming its most-watched series ever. This deadly survival game story introduced a record-breaking number of viewers to Korean content and managed to bag several nominations and awards at Western award shows in the process.

Netflix's arrival on the K-drama scene has also shaken up the traditional production model. For one, the remarkable popularity of *Squid Game* has led to a second season. Fully pre-produced series are also no longer the exception, with the live-shoot model pushed out of favour. The global success of K-drama originals have also inspired American remakes.

The Good Doctor is a US adaptation of the 2013 Korean series of the same name, while American adaptations of *Crash Landing on You* and *Hotel del Luna* are reportedly in the works in 2022. And it's a two-way street. Some of the most popular cable TV and streaming series in Korea are Korean remakes of American and European shows. They include the highest-rated drama in Korean cable TV history, *The World of the Married*, adapted from the UK's BBC series, *Doctor Foster*; *Money Heist: Korea-Joint Economic Area*, based on Netflix's Spanish

series *La Casa de Papel*; and *Suits*, based on the US legal drama of the same name.

Promoting Korea

Much like K-pop, the popularity of K-dramas has elicited an unparalleled interest in Korean culture. These shows offer viewers around the world a window into Korean language, customs, history and food; if a character is eating Korean-style fried chicken on screen, rest assured fans will be next in line to try it.

K-dramas have also proved to be a boon for tourism. In a 2017 survey undertaken by the Korea Tourism Organization, more than half of the country's visitors (polled from the likes of China, Japan, Thailand and the US) said that they travelled to Korea after watching TV dramas and films. One of the biggest hits from 2016, *Descendants of the Sun*, is estimated to have pumped a whopping one trillion won into the Korean economy after the series was sold to more than 30 countries. In the process, it's believed to have attracted 100,000 tourists to Korea, who helped turn some of the drama's filming sites – like a former US military base in Paju – into new tourist destinations.

Between 2015 and 2020, Netflix invested US$700 million into creating Korean content. And where Netflix goes, others follow. Disney+ and Apple TV+ have commissioned original Korean-language productions, including *Snowdrop* (2021) and *Pachinko* (2022) respectively.

Below Filming *Squid Game*

Right Statue of *Winter Sonata* actors Bae Yong-joon and Choi Ji-woo, Nami Island

With this international investment comes change. While plots involving a series of comical misunderstandings will always have their place in K-dramas, writers today are more often than not pushing boundaries with their stories. Be it an exploration of household debt or a look at the exploitation of migrant workers, international audiences are being introduced to contemporary issues plaguing Korean society. And that's exactly what K-drama has always been about: making world-class entertainment from compelling storylines.

Squid Game

While this award-winning series was critically acclaimed around the world, it received mixed reactions in Korea. Some were unimpressed by the predictable tropes and plot devices, including the reunion of long-lost siblings and confrontations between frenemies. It did, however, find fans in older viewers, who felt nostalgic for the old-school kids' games depicted (albeit horrific in their new renditions).

브랜딩과 광고

Branding and advertising

When a TV show breaks for a commercial, there's a good chance the faces staring out at viewers don't change. The use of celebrities as spokespeople is a huge part of advertising, both in print and CF ("commercial films", as Koreans call video ads). Hiring actors and idols to promote everything from cosmetics to school uniforms takes advantage of Korea's strong fandom culture. And it's a strategy that works: when Coway hired K-pop band Girls' Generation to endorse its water purifiers in 2011, sales rose 400 per cent over the previous year.

In return, celebrities get a big payday, often far more than what they make from album sales or TV contracts. In 2021, roughly US\$10.8 million of A-list actor Jun Ji-hyun's US\$12.2 million in earnings came from endorsements. None of this is considered selling out: the public doesn't view a movie star stooping to shill for fried chicken as a stoop at all. The chance to make money endorsing products is seen as something they've earned, and so commercials serve as a popularity thermometer, indicating how successful a celebrity is at any moment.

As Korea's pop culture appeal spreads globally, so does the appetite for Korean celebrity-fronted ads. Korean chaebol are utilizing domestic talent for international campaigns, as seen with Samsung and BLACKPINK, while international corporations are taking advantage of Korean stars' popularity, as McDonald's did when it created the limited-time BTS Meal in 50 countries.

K-pop star-fronted advert in Seoul

The Busan
International Film
Festival, 2016

At the movies

Standing in contrast to the bubblegum-driven music of K-pop, the serious and dark nature of Korean film is a hallmark of the most beloved local film industries in the world.

During the first two decades of the 21st century, Korean cinema – which now includes original streaming content – emerged as Asia's Hollywood. Its readaptation of American film genres, frank depictions of violence and sex, and biting political commentaries contributed to its success globally, first in the niche DVD market before finding a mainstream audience.

Government regulated

Korean cinema, which celebrated the 100th anniversary of its first film premiere in 2019, was born during the Japanese colonial period (1910-1945). Initially, film became a way to respond to the nation's tragedy, with films such as *Arirang* (1926) critiquing Japanese rule

before censorship was tightened. Following the Korean War, cinema entered a golden age, producing over 200 films per year from 1968 to 1971. Colonialism was still at the forefront of storylines, and many films tried to reconcile the family tragedies and traumas of occupation, as well as the Korean War and subsequent division. However, this period of cinema came to a screeching halt in 1972, when Park Chung-hee's military government forced the industry to only make films that were "morally correct". Its artistic expression stifled, South Korean cinema became comparable to that of North Korea.

By the 1980s, things were looking up – on the surface, that is. The new president Chun Doo-hwan introduced

the "3S policy" – Sex, Sports and Screen – which actively encouraged things like nudity and eroticism in film. A win for the industry, perhaps (box offices were booming), but with the government retaining a strong hold on politically sensitive subject matters, this policy offered a slightly false sense of freedom.

Regardless, change was afoot, with a new wave of independent filmmakers and directorial talent taking a rebellious approach. And the European movie circuit was ready for them, with recognition coming in thick and fast. Directors like Jang Sun-woo, Im Kwon-taek and Park Kwang-su began testing the boundaries of censorship, with Park and Jang creating politically motivated films (*Chilsu and Mansu* and *The Age of Success* respectively). In a canny move, they submitted these to the censorship board around the 1988 Seoul Olympics, knowing that the world was watching, and therefore increasing the chance of the films being released – and they were.

Art imitates politics

Politics continued to play its part in the film industry. As a result of the government's transition to democracy in 1987 and, later, the Sunshine Policy era (1998–2007), North Korea became a hot topic for writers. This policy saw the liberal South Korean government take a

soft approach towards North Korea by promoting reconciliation and communication, actively avoiding any use of force and jumpstarting economic cooperation projects between North and South Korea. The film industry was quick to incorporate this as a narrative feature. One of the biggest box office hits during this time was *Shiri* (1999), a thriller in which South Korean agents hunt down a North Korean assassin while the two countries try to reconcile. Another industry-defining film was *JSA* (2000), which centres around an investigation of a shooting at the DMZ; while it ends in bloodshed and dispute, the film sees soldiers from the two sides forming friendships. Rather than villainizing North Koreans, these films showcased the division as the main enemy, and

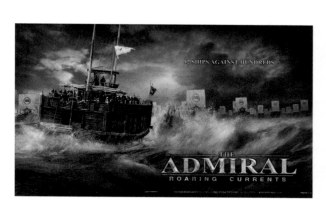

Above Park So-dam and Choi Woo-sik in *Parasite*, 2019

Left Film poster for *The Admiral: Roaring Currents*

were a hit with the South Korean public who were – just like in the rest of the world – continuously talking about North Korea.

Engrossing genres

Aside from North Korea and tackling political intricacies, the subjects that have brought huge cinematic success are historical dramas *(sageuk)* and commentaries on contemporary social and economic problems. If the generic landmarks of Hollywood are aliens, superheroes and the wild west, Korean cinema's iconography is the pre-modern past, best represented in the *sageuk* genre. Though largely unknown in the West, the most commercially successful film in Korea is a *sageuk*, *The Admiral:*

Stars of the industry

Song Kang-ho

A brilliant thespian who has been the face of New Korean Cinema for the past three decades, Song has starred in four of the seven movies directed by Bong Joon-ho, including *Parasite*.

Im Kwon-taek

Known for cinematically representing traditional Korean sentiments, Im is the only director whose life's work spans the golden age of the 1960s, the New Korean Cinema of the 1980s and the blockbuster era of the new millennium.

Hong Sang-soo

The most prolific auteur-director of New Korean Cinema, Hong has made close to 30 films since starting his career in 1996.

Youn Yuh-jung

Youn's film debut was as the femme fatale in the 1971 remake of *The Housemaid*. She won an Academy Award in 2021 – the first for a Korean actor – for Best Supporting Actress.

Roaring Currents (2014). Based on the 1597 Battle of Myeongnyang between Korea and Japan, this movie offers Korean audiences a glimpse of their past glory, brought to life with impressive CGI-generated battle scenes.

While films of the *sageuk* genre rely on historic events set in bygone periods, many of the most popular films of the last decade have been firmly rooted in the present. In 2008, South Korea's government changed once again, bringing in a decade of conservative rule. While this shifted the way that North Korea was depicted on screen – primarily as an antagonistic, volatile country – filmmakers continued to produce movies that pushed boundaries and asked questions on sensitive subjects. Stories of economic struggle and humanity in crisis were suddenly dominating screens

and drawing record-breaking numbers at box offices. Popular progressive films such as *Masquerade* (2012) and *Train to Busan* (2016) – which sees a zombie apocalypse wreak havoc on the safety of the population – sowed the seeds for the eventual production of Bong Joon-ho's modern masterpiece, *Parasite* (2019). Featuring a family of four living in a slum undergoing a battle of survival, *Parasite* portrays the unfair system of capitalism and effectively avoids a happy ending – winning Oscar recognition in the process.

A post-cinema world

Despite the growing challenges of the streaming era and the impact of the COVID-19 pandemic, Korean cinema is still going strong – a testament to the talent at the heart of the industry. And much like K-drama, it has the streaming giant Netflix – which invested US$500 million in Korean contentin 2021 alone – to thank. Pivoting around serious subject matters and visceral violent aesthetics, Korean hit titles are easy to locate on Netflix top ten lists today; this continued desire for content results in continued investment that shows no signs of slowing down. Clearing up at the next awards season? Don't be surprised to see Korean film again.

Graphic poster for 2016 zombie film, *Train to Busan*

Movies through the years

Korean filmmakers have been redefining the landscape of both local and global cinema for decades.

1926

The now lost silent film *Arirang* kickstarts a resilient, anti-colonial period of Korean cinema.

1961

Melodrama/horror film *The Housemaid* is released, later inspiring Bong Joon-ho's *Parasite* (2019).

1999

Action-packed film *Shiri*, about North Korean spies, is arguably the first Korean film to become a hit in Japan.

1988

Chilsu and Mansu – a film about workers trapped on a rooftop – signals cinema's switch to political realism.

2000

Peppermint Candy is the first mainstream movie to deal with the Gwangju Uprising of 1980, where thousands were killed by the military regime.

2003

Oldboy's three-minute corridor fight scene, shot in one continuous take, has a huge impact worldwide and leads to a Hollywood sequel.

2020

Parasite (2019) becomes the first foreign-language film to win the Academy Award's Best Picture prize.

2013

Sci-fi action film *Snowpiercer*, made with mostly Hollywood stars, is released and later adapted into a US TV show.

2006

Monster film *The Host* becomes the highest-grossing film of all time in Korea.

KOREA IS
SHAPING THE FUTURE

Ppalli ppalli ("hurry up") is often among the first expressions that foreigners learn in this fast-paced country, where a need for speed and efficiency drives everything. It's this goal-oriented mindset that has seen Korea grow exponentially – and miraculously – over the last 30 years, from a war-torn country to one that's at the forefront of innovation. Korea's secret? It anticipates the future like nowhere else. For many, a world of robots and AI feels like science fiction of the far future, but in Korea it's a reality, and it's happening now. Add to this one of the world's fastest internet speeds, an ingenious beauty scene and a drive to reshape what life beyond earth could look like one day, and it's safe to say that Korea is well and truly building a new world. What might Korea look like in the next 30 years? It's anyone's guess.

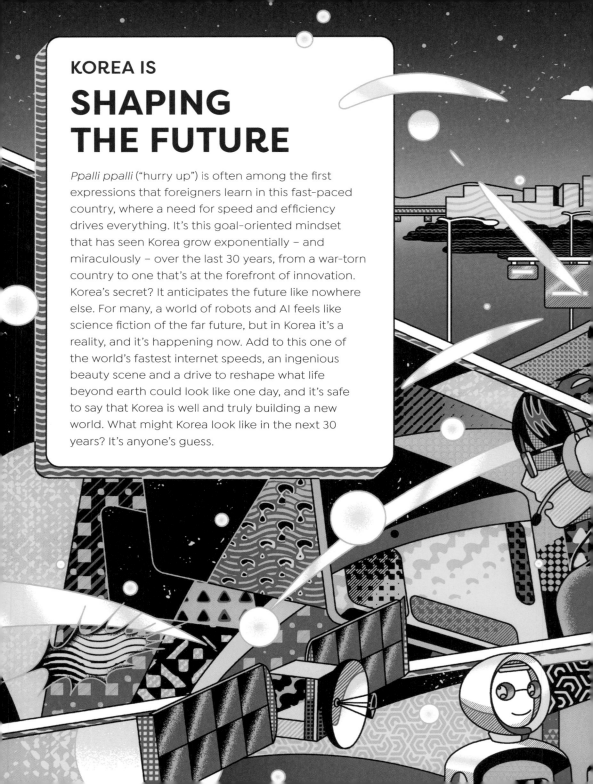

온라인 세계

The online world

Korea is one of the most wired countries on earth. Fast internet speeds are a source of national pride, and have given birth to a rich online culture that's reshaped everyday living.

It's hard to imagine a Korea before the internet. The country has not only created one of the world's fastest internet speeds, but also revolutionized how people connect. In Seoul, free Wi-Fi is ubiquitous, even on subway trains. Smartphone users account for nearly 95 per cent of the population – the majority of whom connect with friends and family through messaging app KakaoTalk – and nearly half of the country are already 5G users.

Dialling in

With its first network launching as early as 1982, Korea has always been at the forefront of the internet world. But it was the government's push to make the country an internet powerhouse that made Korea a world leader.

During his presidency from 1998 to 2003, Kim Dae-jung and his government implemented policy to boost the IT industry and ensure Korea made the best use of its computers. Korea's densely populated cities, coupled with the mountainous geography, made it relatively easy to build broadband infrastructure and make internet connection more accessible – both central to Kim's plans. By 2000, nearly half of Korea was connected, forever changing the way content was consumed and conversations had.

Feeling connected

Today, internet consumption is highly centred around user-generated content. On average, Koreans spend nearly an hour a day on YouTube, watching things like video game playthroughs, make-up tutorials and *gongbang* – "study with me" videos, which have racked up millions of views.

Key to the success of these videos is creating a feeling of connection in an online world. Nowhere is this more evident than in the global pheno-menon of mukbang, which comes from the Korean word *meokda* ("to eat") and *bangsong* ("broadcasting"). Creators and streamers broadcast themselves eating while interacting with viewers – a concept that took many by surprise at first, but soon became popular, especially with those dining at home alone *(p87)*. The word even entered the Oxford English Dictionary in 2021.

Regardless of the type of video, streamers work hard to maintain relationships with their audience. By choosing to live-stream rather than upload a pre-recorded video, streamers can communicate directly with viewers through chat functions, often adapting their entertainment based on comments. And this hard work is rewarded with donations and tips. On AfreecaTV, a peer-to-peer (P2P) video streaming service, viewers send "star balloons" (monetized donations) to streamers as a show of love. In return, some loyal fans expect the streamers to remember their username and treat them specially – something not so dissimilar to K-pop fandom culture (p174). In the world of K-pop, platforms like Weverse also work as a bridge between idols and fans. Idols can broadcast a live stream or write a post, and by cutting out the likes of TV presenters and radio DJs, the relationship between the stars and their fans feels more intimate and personal.

In the game
Arguably Korea's biggest internet community is found in its gaming

Playing e-sports video games at a PC *bang* in Seoul

sphere. In fact, it was the popularity of PC games such as *StarCraft*, a real-time strategy game, in the early 2000s that highlighted the need for faster internet connections among gamers, with providers rushing to meet the demand. PC *bang (p119)* – Korean-style internet cafés where gamers play the latest video games alone or with friends – are ubiquitous across the country. Equipped with state-of-the-art desktops and ergonomic chairs, and priced cheaply, they attract everyone from students to workers. Whether PC *bang* will survive in a post-pandemic and smartphone-led world remains to be seen.

The rise of e-sports

E-sports, however, are unlikely to go anywhere, thanks to successful titles like *League of Legends* and *PlayerUnknown's Battlegrounds*. Long before video gamers started to rack up tens of millions of Korean won by streaming themselves playing games on platforms like Twitch, Koreans were consuming gaming as TV content. In 2000, OGN was launched as the world's first e-sports and gaming-dedicated TV channel. Pro-gamer teams would play *StarCraft*, and viewers would tune in to analyze the style of their favourite gamer and share their opinions online.

Today, e-sports is just as much an established sport in Korea as archery or baseball. Private academies and businesses are willing to sponsor pro-gamers the same way they do sports players. Lim Yo-hwan – one of the most prominent pro-gamers in

E-sports controversy

In 2010, a major match-fixing scandal rocked the Korean e-sports world. A group of people – including professional gamers – were found guilty of rigging the match results of *StarCraft* for an illegal gambling site. It was seen as the first confirmed case in which professional gamers were involved in match fixing and left a stain on the industry's reputation.

the country – signed on with SK Telecom T1 (now T1), a Korean e-sports organization, in 2004. The news made headlines, seen as the beginning of a new era for gaming with more high-paid pro-gamers to come.

Faker (real name Lee Sang-hyeok) was one such gamer: considered to be the best *League of Legends* player of all time, he's won the game's World Championship three times. His fame is recognized outside the gaming community, landing him various advertising deals with the likes of Lotte Confectionery. With an estimated annual salary of millions of dollars, Faker speaks volumes for how big an e-sports market Korea is – one of the largest in terms of revenue and players' earnings, alongside China and the US.

Starting the conversation

The internet, clearly, has a huge role in public discourse. It can make gamers stars and establish relationships between people of vastly different backgrounds, but it can also shape

Internet slang

Selka

Long before "selfie" was named the word of the year in 2013 by the Oxford English Dictionary, Koreans were using *selka* – a portmanteau of "self" and "camera".

Kkk

This is less a word, and more a way to express the sound of laughter when messaging.

Jjal

The Korean word for "meme", *jjal* mostly refers to images that are funny and random.

Heol

This word is used when expressing a form of shock, meaning "no way" or "oh my god".

Kol

Meaning "okay", "sure" or "deal", this word is often used when agreeing to plans, as if to say "I'm in!".

Daebak

Used when celebrating a big win or major news, *daebak* means awesome or amazing.

Above Gamers compete in the 2015 *StarCraft II* ProLeague tournament

Right Playing an AR game in Seoul

the perception of politics or public legislation. While social media platforms such as Facebook and Twitter play a part, Korean forums such as Daum Café lead the conversation. Communities on Daum, for example, have a clear theme and serve a specific audience: within "Women's Generation", women discuss subjects like feminism and politics, while "FM Korea" is where mostly men discuss the likes of football or video games. Viral posts from these groups sometimes make it on the news; in the run-up to the 2022 Korean presidential election, progressive candidate Lee Jae-myung posted on "Women's Generation", pledging to tackle dating violence and take a tougher stance on sexual crime. He didn't win the election, but these online spaces were integral to his campaign, and their influence on current affairs is huge.

Monitoring the web

Given the sizable impact that online discourses have on Korean society, malicious comments – predominantly directed towards women – have long been an issue. Though cyber-bullying is a global problem, its prominence in Korea is tenfold, especially given the dominant role that web portal comment sections play in shaping public opinion.

The issue of cyberbullying has been met with calls for web companies and the government to take action against hostile comments, as well as better moderated social media platforms. One result saw Naver and Daum, two of Korea's most influential web portals, close the comment section for entertainment news.

It's not just keyboard warriors that are a cause for public concern. Gaming might have a huge following and largely be regarded as a hobby, but addiction has been a contentious social issue. The implementation of countermeasures, such as midnight gaming curfews for those aged below 16, aimed to combat this. However, following years of criticism that the policy was government overreach, the curfew was lifted in 2021.

Browsing into the future

So what does the future bring? Already we're seeing steps into the metaverse with advancements in augmented reality (AR) and virtual reality (VR). In 2022, K-pop girl group BLACKPINK teamed up with video

부 캐
Bookae

An "alternative character" or persona, which some people take on for online spaces.

———————————————

game PUBG Mobile to hold its first-ever virtual in-game concert, showcasing 3D avatars of the four band members in post-apocalyptic settings. And this isn't a one-off. VR cafés and gaming dens are shooting up across Seoul, where people can immerse themselves in worlds that have few ties to the everyday. This, surely, is only the start of a life lived virtually. Given Korea's technological prowess and 5G superpowers, it's possible that the metaverse could happen first – successfully – in Korea, with AI robots and holograms one day becoming as ubiquitous as smartphones.

K-웹툰

Korean webtoons

Given how digitally driven Korea is, it's apt that a genre of comics made to be viewed on smartphones was created here. A blend of "web" and "cartoons", webtoons emerged in the early 2000s as a result of the internet boom and financial crisis. With many people unable to afford *manhwa* (paper comics), digital comics – being accessible and cheaper – were a no-brainer.

Part of their success stems from their accessibility. Anyone can upload a webtoon to a forum, with amateurs and budding artists able to bag a big break. Readers share their thoughts in the comments at the end of each weekly episode; in turn, creators often make revisions to future episodes. Two of the biggest platforms and apps are

WEBTOON and Kakao Webtoon. Initially known as Daum Webtoon, Kakao was the world's first webtoon platform when it launched in 2003. Hot on its heels in 2004 was WEBTOON, now the world's largest digital comics platform, with over 72 million users across 100 countries.

Most people will know webtoons without even realizing. Their vibrant visuals and eclectic genres, ranging from rom-coms to sci-fi thrillers, have influenced big K-dramas. The likes of *Hellbound* (2021) and *All of Us Are Dead* (2022) are based on Korean webtoons, and much of their success stems from existing fanbases. The surge in global interest for webtoons is so huge that it's become a multi-million-dollar industry in Korea.

Cartoons drawn by webtoon artist Seok-Woo

Using an augmented
reality tool to choose
make-up shades

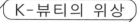

K-뷰티의 위상

A beauty takeover

If there's a new trend in the global beauty world, chances are it started in Korea. Here, standards of beauty are narrow, resulting in a rapidly innovating industry.

Korea is the world's third-largest cosmetics exporter, behind France and the US – fitting for a country with precise ideals about beauty *(p62)* and the technological skill to meet them.

Creating an industry

As K-pop and K-dramas grew in popularity in the 2010s, so did the aesthetic of the Korean celebrity. When concepts like sheet masks, essence, serum and cushion foundations first made appearances in the West, they were received with scepticism, even a bit of amusement. But with some of the biggest Korean celebrities working as ambassadors for top Korean skincare brands, the global market began to take note. Soon enough, high street and luxury brands were releasing copycat products inspired by the Korean market. K-beauty, as it was termed, had arrived.

A different approach

K-beauty is best understood as a preventative, rather than a reactive, process. Kids are taught early about the importance of good skin health: sunscreen and moisturizers are applied religiously, and considered as vital for self-care as brushing the teeth. Later in life, the focus on skincare over make-up aligns with the preference for natural beauty. Generally, eye make-up is kept to a minimum (smoky looks and bold colours are rare), and berry-stained lips are meant to mimic a youthful appearance. If skin is healthy, hydrated and well-balanced, make-up can be used less as a mask and more as an enhancer. And that's where skincare regimens like the 10-step routine *(p208)* come in.

It follows that products centre on raw, natural ingredients, from both plants and animals. Part of K-beauty's global success is introducing the West

Popular products

BB cream

Invented by a German dermatologist, the blemish balm became a phenomenon after being reformulated in Korea as a vitamin-enriched alternative to foundation.

Cushion foundation

Loved for its sheer formulas, this skincare, sunscreen and liquid foundation in compact form was invented by Korean cosmetics giant Amorepacific.

Multi-balm stick

These giant lip balms for the face have become popular as hygienic, contactless, portable touch-up sticks that glide onto cheeks for an instant glow.

Essences, serums and ampoules

This trio of products is a key part of the 10-step skincare routine, with each more potent and viscous than the last. Essence is a watery solution, ampoules contain super-charged ingredients and serums fall between the two.

Above Popular K-beauty products, renowned for their cute, colourful packaging

Right Production line at an Amore-pacific factory

to new, surprising ingredients. While some – such as snail slime, great for plumping – aren't Korean inventions, the country has reformulated and propelled them to stardom. Others draw on beloved Korean techniques; fermented skincare ingredients — be it berries, rice, yeast, ginseng or soybeans – are said to be more potent, penetrate deeper and help strengthen ageing skin.

Outside of home care, monthly and even weekly visits to dermatologists for a facial are common. One of the most popular procedures is the skin booster shot, a form of microneedling that injects vitamins and nutrients into the skin and penetrates deep into its layers. The trademarked Rejuran Healer is a gamechanger, an injectable based on salmon DNA that was developed by a Korean pharmaceutical company and is said to improve skin elasticity.

Next-generation skincare

Beyond pioneering ingredients, Korea leads the way in high-tech skincare. For starters, many brands combine AI with facial detection technology: contactless diagnostic tools that assess skin condition and skincare needs, both in-store and through mobile apps. A quick scan of the face is all that's needed to generate an in-depth analysis of moisture levels, hyperpigmentation, problem areas or pore size. Customers are then provided with a list of optimal products to address their skincare concerns.

A similar approach is taken for make-up. At some stores, gone are the days when customers leave with half a dozen lipstick swatches striping the back of their hands. Today, augmented reality-powered mirrors allow customers to snap a photo and try on different shades of lipsticks, eyeshadow and foundation without touching their face. Virtual make-up try-ons are also available online, so consumers can test shades and place an order without leaving the house.

Better yet, specially designed 3D printing systems developed in Korea can print out sheet masks that align perfectly with different facial features. After first capturing individual facial dimensions – be it the space between the eyes, the length of the nose or the area of the cheeks – 3D printing machines will create a personalized hydrogel mask.

Given its forward-thinking prowess, Korea is arguably on its way to being the world's leading cosmetics exporter. But with the rising backlash against Korea's exacting beauty standards (p62), not to mention the nature of an industry that sees trends come and go famously fast, the K-beauty world needs to evolve.

10단계 루틴

10-step routine

Contrary to popular belief, the concept of a 10-step Korean skincare routine is a distinctly American one. The term was coined by a Korean American K-beauty expert while explaining Korean skincare to American journalists, for whom the idea of using more than five products a day was a novel concept. In Korea, what's now known as the 10-step skincare routine in the West is simply a matter of good skin hygiene and doesn't go by a specific name.

This now famed routine is about layering products in an order that makes sense, with lighter products applied first and heavier moisturisers and oils applied last. In the morning, that might look like a light cleanser, toner, an essence, serum or ampoule, moisturizer and sunscreen. At night, the routine starts with a double cleanse, and can be followed by as few or as many steps as time and skin needs allow: exfoliator toner, targeted treatments (from acne to anti-wrinkle), sheet mask and moisturizer. In other words, the typical skincare routine is not set in stone: not everyone follows every step or treatment, but rather tailors their routine to their own skincare needs. The overall aim? Korea's famous "glass skin" effect: a bouncy, hydrated, dewy complexion.

Skincare minimalism (or skinimalism), in which routines are pared down to four basic products, has emerged in the West in reaction to this multi-step routine. But in Korea, the concept of a 10-step beauty routine was never a fad or a trend. It's simply a lifestyle.

Skincare products at a Nature Republic store

Technology titans

Home to some of the world's largest tech companies, Korea is at the very forefront of modern innovation, pioneering developments from smart cities to the metaverse.

Glossy, fast-paced and decidedly future-oriented, the tech scene is a window into the country's neophilia, or love of the new. This drives Korea's relentless progress, as the demand for cutting-edge electronics and digitized convenience shows no sign of abating.

Finding its footing

When the Korean War ended in 1953, Korea was a primarily agrarian economy lagging behind the industrialized North. Over the next few decades, family-run chaebol (p70) like Samsung drove a period of lightning-fast economic growth, known as the "Miracle on the Han River". Today, Korea is the tenth largest economy in the world, and Samsung Electronics alone accounts for a fifth of the country's total exports. And that's not forgetting its digital superpower: Korea has nearly 100 per cent broadband coverage, and was first in the world to commercially roll out 5G nationwide in 2019.

Changing lives

An abundance of home-grown electronics, advanced internet infrastructure and high digital literacy has made Korea a utopia of technological convenience. Flip-top refrigerators are designed to store kimchi at optimal temperatures for up to a year. At cashierless convenience stores, ready-made meal kits are available around the clock, and online retailers offer breakneck deliveries of everything from groceries to fast fashion.

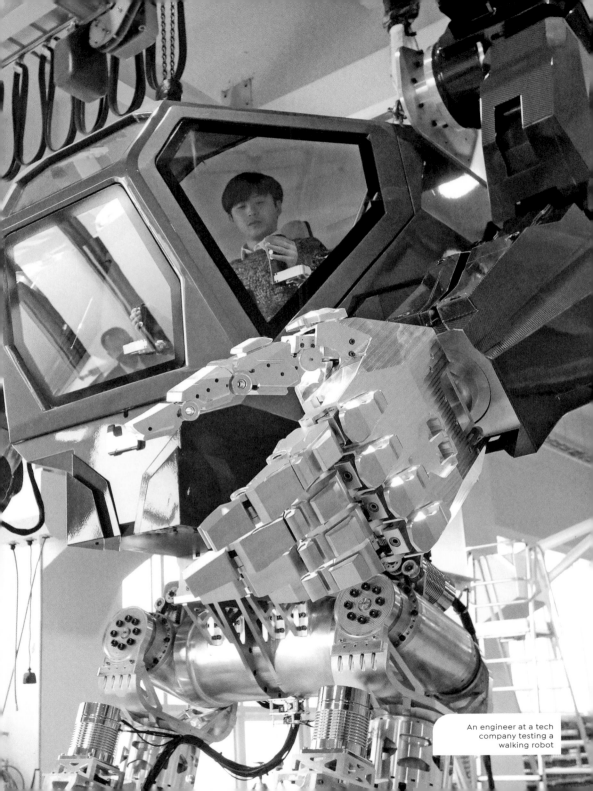

An engineer at a tech
company testing a
walking robot

With the country's smartphone penetration rate at almost 100 per cent, tasks like renewing a driver's licence have been made instantly accessible on government apps. The dominance of virtual wallets that can be used anywhere, helped in large part by Wi-Fi being within easy reach in urban areas, have also rendered cash a relic of the past. The modern smartphone is now utterly integral to the country's obsession with instant convenience.

Looking to the future

Fittingly for a country that routinely tops global innovation indices, Korean tech companies are leaping headfirst into next-generation technologies. Some of the country's brightest innovators envisage a future in which vital issues like climate change are targeted through an ever-expanding digital ecosystem. Hyundai Motor,

A self-regulating smart farm in Seoul

whose leader Chung Eui-sun believes that personal robots will one day become as ubiquitous as mobile phones, is dreaming up a world populated by intelligent machines. Samsung, meanwhile, is expanding beyond smartphones into bio-technology and artificial intelligence.

Urban experiments taking place across Korea offer an intriguing glimpse into the cities of tomorrow. Ulsan, an industrial hub known for shipyards and oil refineries, is also the testbed for hydrogen-powered cities, trialling fuel cell buses, boats and taxis. Jeju Island is pushing forward with plans to fully replace all petrol automobiles with electric vehicles by 2030, while experimenting with new infrastructure to safely support self-driving vehicles.

Outside of major cities, the government is promoting self-regulating smart farms. They hope these will entice younger city-dwellers into taking up farming, helping to repopulate rapidly shrinking rural communities. Digital governance is on the rise, too, with government agencies like the Korean Customs Service creating blockchain platforms to fight customs fraud.

When it comes to technological experimentation, it's clear that nothing is off limits. With some of the world's most inventive technological pioneers, Korea is truly laying down the blueprints for a tech-reliant future.

Remarkable feats of technology

From AI-versus-human showdowns to the world's first intelligent city, the history of Korean technology is full of the brilliant, the groundbreaking and the provocative.

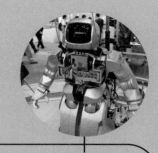

1998
MPMan, the first portable mp3 music player in the world, is released by SaeHan Information Systems.

2005
Scientists at the Korea Advanced Institute of Science and Technology create Hubo, the world's second humanoid robot.

2012
A prison in the city of Pohang hires the world's first robot prison warden.

2009
CJ Group opens the first 4D movie theatre in Seoul, later exporting the technology worldwide.

2012
Tesco Homeplus opens the world's first virtual grocery store on an underground subway platform in Seoul.

2015
Korean scientists create an Afghan hound named Snuppy, the first dog clone in the world.

2020
Korean broadcaster MBN debuts the country's first AI news anchor, modelled on announcer Kim Ju-ha.

2019
Korea is the first country to roll out a 5G network and Samsung releases the world's first 5G smartphone.

2015
Songdo, the world's first smart city, is completed atop 600 ha (1500 acres) of land reclaimed from the sea.

1 Samsung's innovative curve display

2 An LG home-brewing kit

3 The Alpha Mini robot

4 Virtual musician Rhea Keem

5 Songdo smart city

For a country so small that it might be missed on the map, Korea has a vast technological footprint. From smartphones to coffee-serving robots, examples of Korean technology can be found everywhere.

Smartphones

Before K-pop, Korea's most recognizable export was smartphones, and here Samsung reigns supreme. In addition to innovations like the world's first curved display or the first foldable smartphone, the company has also supplied many of the components – such as displays or semiconductors – that go into its main competitor's flagship product, the iPhone.

Appliances

In a country where improvements to everyday domestic routines are as celebrated as breakthrough technologies, even the most humble household appliance undergoes constant reinterpretation. Based on the belief that every small inconvenience has an elegant technological solution, LG rules over the home appliance market, with products like a vacuum cleaner that empties out its own dust collector, or a capsule beer machine that brews five different types of beer at the push of a button.

Robotics

In Korea, which has the highest number of industrial robots per capita in the world, robots are infused with both a sense of utilitarian convenience and whimsical fun. Consider the Alpha Mini, a doll-sized robot used as a teaching aid at childcare centres in Seoul. Service robots are rapidly becoming part of the urban landscape, too. At automated cafés around the country, robot baristas with names like "Baris" make lattes, while robot servers deliver drinks to customers.

Artificial Intelligence

A world where humans coexist with their artificial counterparts is fast becoming reality. AI-powered virtual avatars are working as bank clerks, television announcers and celebrities. Rozy, a virtual influencer, dances on insurance ads, while LG's virtual musician Rhea Keem is writing her own songs for a debut album. Some AI celebrities are even getting acting deals.

Smart cities

Following Songdo, the smart city where pneumatic tubes – not garbage trucks – whisk away residents' trash, Korea has been on a mission to bestow high-tech convenience on all of its cities. Seoul was the first city in the world to join the metaverse in 2021, unveiling plans to bring municipal services and cultural events to a virtual public community. At Eco Delta Village, a smart city pilot project in the harbour city of Busan, every resident wears a smartwatch that connects them to their home's digital network. In exchange for living rent-free, residents allow the companies running the project to collect and use their data in order to make improvements.

Engineering marvels

Korea is in perpetual motion: constructing next-generation container ships, building new cities, launching satellites into space. And it's all thanks to a deep pool of engineering talent.

Korea isn't simply shaping the future – arguably, it *is* the future. Engineers working in more than 7,200 companies are driving progress both within Korea and beyond, developing infrastructure that keeps the world moving.

On land and at sea

The Korean engineering most people are familiar with is the four-wheeled kind. Hyundai is a global name, and with its sister corporation, Kia, it's nearly single-handedly turned Korea into the world's fifth-largest car producer. But its prowess extends far beyond SUVs. Its subsidiary Hyundai Rotem makes bullet trains, which reach speeds of 305 km/h (190 mph) and can travel from Seoul to Busan – a distance of 325 km (202 miles) – in 2 hours and 9 minutes.

Hyundai is also a major player in an often overlooked industry: shipbuilding. While Korea didn't start making ships

until 1968, it controls more than one third of the industry today, and is home to the world's four biggest shipbuilders. Considering that 90 per cent of traded goods are transported by ship, it's not a stretch to say that Korean engineers are responsible for building the global supply chain.

Korean firms are also at the fore of making international shipping more environmentally friendly. In 2022, Korea's shipyards accounted for more than half of all orders for eco-friendly ships, be they powered by batteries or alternative fuels. Hyundai, Daewoo and Samsung are also working to develop ships powered by ammonia, a possible future green fuel.

In the air

Alongside Korea's major shipyards are more than 100 companies specializing in aviation, aircraft mechanics and

Above The Nuri rocket launching from the Naro Space Center in 2022

Right KTX high-speed bullet train at a station in Seoul

assembly. Many of the parts that these aviation businesses manufacture go to Korean Air and Korea Aerospace Industries; in turn, these companies develop aircraft, such as unmanned aerial vehicles.

Korea is forever aiming higher. In 2022, it launched five satellites into orbit on its Nuri rocket, made domestically with contributions from some 300 Korean companies. According to the Korea Aerospace Research Institute, this made the national space programme just the seventh to develop a space launch vehicle able to carry a satellite in excess of one ton. The Nuri satellites will spend up to two

years monitoring the atmosphere and performing other observation missions.

The next step for Korean aerospace engineers is to go beyond Earth's orbit. In a partnership with NASA, Korea is expected to launch its first lunar orbiter, and it's also working towards sending probes to the moon. Meanwhile, Kia and Hyundai are working with six Korean research institutes to develop tools that will improve how astronauts travel across the moon. When one considers how rapidly the country's engineering prowess has developed over the past half-century, it surely won't be long before Korea is looking past the moon, to Mars and beyond.

Index

Acknowledgments

DK Eyewitness would like to thank the following people for their contributions to this project:

Ann Babe is a South Korean-born and US-based journalist whose writings on Korea have appeared in *The New York Times*, *Wired*, *Kinfolk* and beyond. When in Korea, you'll find her hiking, eating *tteokbokki* and swearing off soju for the umpteenth time.

Matthew C Crawford is a Canadian writer who has written about Korea for the BBC and *South China Morning Post*, among others. His love for mountains has seen him climb peaks in Bolivia, India and Nepal, and he's still working away at the 7,715 mountains of his adopted home, Korea.

Yim Hyun-su is a Seoul-based journalist whose reporting has featured in *The Washington Post* among others. During his time as a reporter at *The Korea Herald*, the largest English-language newspaper in Korea, Yim covered internet culture and the entertainment industry.

Iris (Yi Youn) Kim is a Seoul-born writer living in Los Angeles. Her work – which mostly covers Asian American identity, politics and culture – has appeared in *Salon*, *Slate*, *TIME*, *Delish* and *Business Insider*. Iris is a 2022 PEN America Emerging Voices Fellow, and a Center for Public Diplomacy US-South Korea NextGen Creative Fellow.

Kyung Hyun Kim is a creative writer, film producer and scholar, as well as a professor in the Department of East Asian Studies at UC Irvine, California. He has authored numerous books, including *Hegemonic Mimicry: Korean Popular Culture of the Twenty-First Century* (2021), and has co-produced and co-scripted two award-winning feature films, *Never Forever* (2007) and *The Housemaid* (2010).

Max Kim has lived and studied in Germany, the UK and the US, and now resides in Seoul. While his writing on technology has been published in newspapers and magazines such as *The Guardian* and *MIT Technology Review*, Max considers himself far more technologically challenged than he would care to admit.

Soo Kim is a Korean journalist based in London and the author of *How to Live Korean* (2020). A former travel writer and commissioning editor at *The Daily Telegraph*, she now regularly reports on the likes of Korean entertainment, health and psychology for *Newsweek*. She's interviewed some of Korea's biggest stars, from *Squid Game* actors to major film directors.

Cecilia Hae-Jin Lee is a Los Angeles-based food and travel writer, photographer and producer. She's an expert on Korean and Mexican art, culture and cuisine, having written cookbooks and travel guides for both. Ask her who invented the Korean taco – she'll know.

Colin Marshall is a Seoul-based writer who has contributed essays on cities, culture and other subjects to publications including *The New Yorker*, *The Guardian* and the *Los Angeles Review of Books*, whose Korea blog he wrote for six years.

Dr Chuyun Oh is a Korean dance theorist and a university professor in the US. She is the author of *K-pop Dance: Fandoming Yourself on Social Media* (2022), and likes to tour dance studios in Seoul to learn trendy K-pop moves (often ending up with muscle cramps).

Vivian Song is a Korean Canadian journalist living in Paris, where she produces food, travel and culture features for publications including *The New York Times*, *CNN* and *Bloomberg*. Since becoming a French citizen, she has made a concerted effort to reconnect with her Korean heritage, and feels anxious when her fridge is low on kimchi.

Charles Usher is an American writer and editor who spent 13 years living in Korea. He's the author of the book *Seoul Sub-urban* (2017) and has written for *The Guardian* and Lonely Planet, among other outlets. He lives in Milwaukee with his wife, Soyi, and their dog, Bono.

Hahna Yoon is a Seoul-based journalist who writes about food, travel and culture for such publications as *The New York Times* and *National Geographic*. When she's not writing, you'll find her cuddling with her puppy, Hodu.

About the illustrator:
Jinhwa Jang is an illustrator from Seoul whose work has appeared in *Bloomberg Businessweek*, *The New York Times*, *The New Yorker* and *Wired*. Jinhwa's illustrations are inspired by the various cities she's lived in – including Hanoi, Shanghai and New York – and the people she's met along the way. Aside from illustrating, she loves spending time walking her dog.

The publisher would like to thank the following for their kind permission to reproduce their photographs:

(Key: a-above; b-below/bottom; c-centre; f-far; l-left; r-right; t-top)

123RF.com: searagen 128

akg-images: Roland and Sabrina Michaud 64-65, 154, 158, 162

Alamy Stock Photo: Aflo Co. Ltd. 186-187, Amanda Ahn 78bl, Chema Grenda Cuti 94-95, Bob Daemmrich 55, Pavel Dudek 14tl, Richard Ellis 30-31br, Everett Collection Inc 178tr, 182-183, 190, 191, Sang Taek Jang / EyeEm 76tc, GRANGER - Historical Picture Archive 33tr, Hemis 130-131tc, Heritage Image Partnership Ltd 42bl, 133cl, David Hodges 176bl, Imaginechina Limited 178tl, Inigo Bujedo Aguirre-VIEW 86, Lucas Jackson / REUTERS 32, Joonsoo Kim 157, Kish Kim / Sipa USA 116, 117, Koshiro K 14cr, Magnolia Pictures / Everett Collection Inc 33cl, Marevision / Agefotostock 112bl, Nippon News / Aflo Co. Ltd. / Alamy Stock Photo 165, JeongHyeon Noh 52, David Parker 27tr, Photo 12 193bc, Pictures From History / CPA Media Pte Ltd 53, 58, Jo Yong Hak / Reuters 43, REUTERS 205, Michael Runkel 18, Seung Il Ryu / ZUMA Press, Inc. 60, Soularue / Hemis.fr 118-119tc, Oran Tantapakul 6-7bc, TCD / Prod.DB 178bl, 193tr, 193cl, VTR 26bl, BJ Warnick / Newscom 33br, 66, BJ Warnick / Yonhap / Newscom 106tr, ZUMA Press, Inc. 188-189

Bridgeman Images: Leonard de Selva 108bl

d'strict: WAVE by d'strict 132

Dreamstime.com: Chanchai Duangdoosan 20-21, F11photo 145, Panya Khamtuy 213br, 214bl, Kidloverz22 14cl, Byungsuk Ko 138, Sungbok Lee 22-23, Jeonghyeon Noh 130tl, Sanga Park 140tr, Yooran Park 81br, Isabel Poulin 28cl, Tawatchai Prakobkit 112tl, 112br, Ika Rahma 96bl, Panwasin Seemala 106tl, Studioclover 112tr,

Tea 208-209, Wing Ho Tsang 134-135, Vikaabdullina 206-207tc, Julien Viry 91, Rangsiya Yanvarat 61tc, Suksan Yodyiam 185

eyevine: Chang W. Lee / New York Times / Redux 114-115, An Rong / New York Times / Redux 175

Getty Images: Atlantide Phototravel 44, Photography by Simon Bond 85, Bride Lane Library / Popperfoto 30tl, Simon Bruty / Anychance 122cl, SeongJoon Cho / Bloomberg 98, 109, 200, 201, 207tr, Jean Chung / Bloomberg 68, 171br, CORR / AFP 122tr, David Ducoin / Gamma-Rapho 19, Jean Guichard / Gamma-Rapho 177, Dallas and John Heaton 129, IOC Olympic Museum / Allsport 143, Insung Jeon / Moment Open 49, Park Ji-Hwan / AFP 213cl, Ed Jones / AFP 104-105, 119tr, 124tr, 198, JTBC PLUS / ImaZinS Editorial 169tc, 169tr, Korea Aerospace Research Institute 216-217tc, Kevin Mazur / WireImage 169c, Timothy Norris 168, Andie Nurhadiyanto / EyeEm 57, Flash Parker / Moment 28br, Pictures from History / Universal Images Group 27cr, Justin Setterfield 124tl, Justin Shin 155, 163, Jessica Solomatenko 130cl, Javier Soriano / AFP 124cl, Matthew Stockman 122br, Chung Sung-Jun 36-37tc, 61br, 67, 72-73tc, 106bl, 106br, 124cr, 210-211, 212, 213tr, Chung Sung-Jun / Stringer 46-47cr, Suntill / Imazins 45, Ten Asia / Multi-Bits 164, The Chosunilbo JNS / Imazins 171tc, THE FACT / Imazins 169br, Universal History Archive / Universal Images Group 33tc, Sayan Uranan / EyeEm 12-13, Anthony Wallace / AFP 82-83, 124bl, 172-173, 214cl, Westend61 140tl, Kevin Winter 166-167, JUNG YEON-JE / AFP 61bl, 62-63, 150-151, 202-203

Getty Images / iStock: Avigator Photographer 6-7, Vittoria Che 196, CJNattanai 140cr, George Clerk 72tl, GoranQ 36tl, 140br, Sungsu Han 81bl, Yeongsik Im 38-39, Wonseok Jang 101, July7th 110, NeoPhoto 14tr, Leo Patrizi / E+ 69, TopPhotoImages 90bl

Greysuitcase: Angela Wijaya 96br, 146

Courtesy of the Gwangju Biennale Foundation: Eeva-Kristiina Harlin and Outi Pieski, Máttaráhku ládjogahpir – Foremother's Hat of Pride, 2017–ongoing. Installation view at 'Minds Rising Sprits Tuning', the 13th Gwangju Biennale, 2021 14bl, Politician Kim Dae-jung, President of the Republic of Korea 1998-2003, viewing Nam June Paik's Dolmen, 1995, at the 1st Gwangju Biennale, 1995 133bc

Mijoo Kim: 24-25

Korea Tourism Organization: Joshua L. Davenport 106cr, Min Hyekyung / VisitKorea.or.kr 111tr, Kim Jiho 96tl

LG Electronics: LG 214cr

The Metropolitan Museum of Art: Water-moon Avalokiteshvara, unidentified artist, Goryeo dynasty (918–1392), Korea, hanging scroll; ink and color on silk. Charles Stewart Smith Collection, Gift of Mrs. Charles Stewart Smith, Charles Stewart Smith Jr., and Howard Caswell Smith, in memory of Charles Stewart Smith, 1914 133tr

Netflix: Noh Juhan 6bl, 180-181, 184, Netflix 178br

Samsung Electronics: © 2010-2022 SAMSUNG 70-71, 214tl

Shutterstock.com: Artyooran 217tr, Becky's 78tl, BUGNUT23 120-121, Jack Dempsey / AP 214tr, Brent Hofacker 78tr, Chuck Hsu 81cr, Yeongsik Im 159, Kim Chon Kil / AP 59, Wesley Kiou 81cl, Steven KJ Lee 81tl, LEEDDONG 50-51, Diego Mariottini 34-35, Sanga Park 16-17, Yooran Park / Artyooran 78br, Pkphotograph 139, Leonardo Spencer 88-89, Street style photo 152-153, Surachat Treekidakorn 26-27tc, TTLSC 87, YONHAP / EPA-EFE / Shutterstock 92-93, Julie Yoon / AP 197, Faiz Zaki 192

Simon & Schuster: Book Cover Image: Kim Jiyoung, Born 1982 149

Mark Parren Taylor: 2-3, 14br, 23tr, 54, 56, 81tr, 84, 96tr, 96cl, 96cr, 136-137, 140cl

Unsplash: Photo by Daniel Bernard 144

Wavepoetry.com: from Yi Sang: Selected Works (Wave Books, 2020) 148

Wikimedia Commons: Unknown author, Public domain 28tc

All other images © Dorling Kindersley

Romanization

The Korean in this book is presented in *Hangeul* script, the official writing system of South Korea. For phrases with no appropriate literal translations, liberal translations or common loanwords have been used. The pronunciation for Korean words given is shown in Revised Romanization, the most common method of expressing *Hangeul* characters in the English language. In some instances, however, exceptions to Revised Romanization have been made for clarity, such as for the names of well-known locations.

Korean names

Family names come before the first names in Korea, a convention followed in this book. Hyphens are used in names where required. However, exceptions to both rules have been made in the case of personal preferences. Depending on the geographical region and the individual, the same family name can often be spelled many different ways; this book adheres to the most common spellings.

Use of Korea

"Korea" is used to represent South Korea throughout this book, unless it is unclear whether the text is referring to North Korea or South Korea, when this custom will be broken for sense purposes.

This book was made with Forest Stewardship Council™ certified paper – one small step in DK's commitment to a sustainable future. **For more information go to www.dk.com/our-green-pledge**

MIX
Paper | Supporting responsible forestry
FSC™ C018179
www.fsc.org

A note from the publisher
World events occur and policies and trends change or evolve at a rapid pace. Every effort has been made to ensure this book is accurate and up-to-date, so if you notice we've got something wrong or left something out, we want to hear about it. Please get in touch at travelguides@dk.com

| Penguin Random House

Senior Editor Zoë Rutland
Project Art Editor Jordan Lambley
Editors Alex Pathe, Bella Talbot, Lucy Sara-Kelly
Designers Ben Hinks, Stuart Tolley
Proofreader Stephanie Smith
Indexer Hilary Bird
Korean Language Consultants Sunhee Jin, Dalyoung Kim, Yeon Jeong Kim
Senior Cartographic Editor Casper Morris
Picture Researcher Claire Guest
Publishing Assistant Halima Mohammed
Illustrator Jinhwa Jang
Jacket Designer Ben Hinks
Production Manager Pankaj Sharma
Senior Production Editor Jason Little
Senior Production Controller Samantha Cross
Managing Editor Hollie Teague
Managing Art Editor Sarah Snelling
Art Director Maxine Pedliham
Publishing Director Georgina Dee

First published in Great Britain in 2023
by Dorling Kindersley Limited
DK, One Embassy Gardens, 8 Viaduct Gardens,
London, SW11 7BW.

The authorised representative in the EEA is
Dorling Kindersley Verlag GmbH. Arnulfstr. 124,
80636 Munich, Germany.

Copyright © 2023 Dorling Kindersley Limited
A Penguin Random House Company
10 9 8 7 6 5 4 3 2
009-335463-Jun/2023

A CIP catalog record for this book is available from the British Library.
A catalog record for this book is available from the Library of Congress.

ISBN: 978 0 2416 1739 7

Printed and bound in Slovakia

For the curious
www.dk.com